I0446442

Contents

Introduction

Employee disengagement is a pressing issue, with around 85% of workers feeling disconnected from their jobs. We will learn cutting-edge coaching techniques, frameworks, and tools to enhance employee engagement, foster growth, and transition from a directive leadership style (a common reason for employee departures) to a coaching-oriented management approach (a key factor in retaining talent).

Many Nobel Prize winners and Olympians were mentored by previous laureates or medalists, showcasing the power of mentorship. You too can become someone who brings out the best in your team members, helping them achieve remarkable success. If you aspire to be the person who nurtures winners, this book is for you.

The workplace was already evolving rapidly, but the global pandemic accelerated this transformation like never before. Leaders and managers are now facing unprecedented rates of change. If you are in a leadership role, you have encountered unfamiliar challenges in the past year. To emerge stronger from this, learn how to coach your team on the skills required in our rapidly changing workplace. We will learn how to coach your teams through the current challenges and changes.

As a business leader, have you ever wished your team could better anticipate problems and maintain focus on the big picture amidst their day-to-day tasks? Strategic thinking skills are highly valuable yet often lacking among professionals. In today's complex and volatile world, leaders grapple with developing their teams' strategic thinking abilities. Coaching can enhance your team's capacity for gaining fresh insights, considering multiple perspectives, and building the skills required for forward-thinking, alignment, prioritization, and maintaining focus on critical matters. Are you prepared to learn how to cultivate a team of strategic thinkers who can streamline decision-making and make your life easier?

Mastering virtual coaching may not be intuitive, but it is a skill that can be acquired. We will guide you in connecting with your team and coaching them effectively in remote settings. Coaching employees virtually may seem daunting due to some challenges. First, there are technical issues and distractions during virtual sessions. The need for scheduling coaching meetings is more critical since spontaneous interactions are rare. Building trust without in-person interactions is challenging. Misunderstandings can occur more easily in virtual communication. Despite these challenges, with practice and the tools we will discuss, you can enhance your skills and confidence as a remote manager and coach.

Think back to your first day at your current job. How did your manager make the transition smoother, and was there something you wish they had done differently, like providing more coaching and support? Onboarding new hires involves more than giving them a company handbook and expecting them to start working immediately. As it sets the tone for the employee's experience, effective onboarding can significantly increase retention. By using a coaching approach, you can help new hires create a vision for their role and the organization, shifting the focus from paperwork and procedures to curiosity and deep listening.

As a people manager, you face the constant challenge of balancing limited time and resources with the never-ending demand for results. You must achieve targets, inspire your team, and manage it all, even in the face of changing strategies and new projects. We will focus on three types of coaches: those seeking performance improvement, those working on career development, and high-performing individuals. Each group comes with its own strengths and challenges, and, as you know, things can get messy sometimes. You will explore scenarios where a coach helps individuals overcome challenges like poor customer service, making difficult career decisions, and dealing with conflict. We will cover topics like assessing coachability, enhancing accountability, and using advanced listening and intuition to drive performance and results.

Chapter 1 Coaching and Developing Employees

Busting myths and finding time

I will help you dispel common coaching myths to become an effective manager and coach. Take Susan, a senior VP aiming for the COO role. Her command-and-control style hindered progress, and she believed coaching was just handholding – a myth we'll debunk. Coaching is not doing the work; it is setting clear expectations, guiding, questioning, and inspiring ownership.

Myth two: "No time for coaching." Yet, Susan's lack of coaching caused wasted time backtracking and extinguishing fires. Coaching fosters collaboration, autonomy, and efficiency. It saves time and boosts results.

Myth three: "Growing employees leads to losing them." Research shows employees leave bad managers, not growth opportunities. Developing your team creates value for all.

Myth four: "Career development is solely the employee's responsibility." But coaching can engage disengaged employees and elevate high potentials.

Promise yourself to let go of these myths. Identify individuals to help grow and protect time for coaching. Start small, experiment, and transform your leadership approach.

Overcoming bias in coaching

If you are a white, male engineer born in the United States, working in a San Francisco tech company, chances are you've chosen people similar to yourself. It's a natural inclination, rooted in unconscious bias, where we tend to favor those who resemble us.

To become a successful coach and leader, it is crucial to be aware of your biases – we all have them. These biases affect not only race and gender but also various other aspects like appearance, education, and more. Systemic bias contributes to the quitting epidemic, as people leave due to stagnant careers and a lack of promotion opportunities. This turnover is emotionally and financially costly, despite evidence showing that diverse workplaces are more engaged, productive, and profitable.

If your organization experiences high turnover, it is not just the organization they are leaving; they might be leaving you. It is time to make more inclusive choices. Review your coaching selections and consider what changes or additions are necessary. If you're a hiring manager, contemplate how you can enhance team diversity.

Establishing a coaching relationship

The three key aspects of coaching relationships: clarity, commitment, and confidentiality. Think about the individuals you've chosen to coach on your team. Some may be high-potentials ready to contribute more, while others might be disengaged and in need of a turnaround. Regardless of where they fall on the engagement spectrum, remember this: your team members seek clarity regarding opportunities, recognition for their skills, and a path to promotion. This is why the first "C" is clarity.

Clarity involves specifying the reasons behind your actions and your team members' career aspirations. Your role is to communicate organizational and team goals, demonstrating how they relate to individual expectations and deliverables. This sets the foundation for progress measurement. Gaining clarity from your team involves asking questions about their career goals and learning desires.

The second "C" is commitment. It entails expressing your intention to make coaching conversations a regular practice and agreeing on logistical details, signifying your dedication to your team's growth and success. Logistics may include meeting days, times, frequency, and location. Consistency in your meeting schedule creates momentum and saves time by avoiding constant scheduling coordination.

The third "C" is confidentiality. To establish trust in coaching, ensure that your conversations remain confidential. Although you may need to share progress highlights with your manager or leadership, the content of your discussions must be held in strict confidence. Explicitly state your commitment to confidentiality.

Cornerstones of coaching

The coaching process is anchored by three core principles: curiosity, letting the employee take the lead, and coaching the whole person. These principles make your conversations more effective.

For example, consider Christy, a team leader facing performance challenges. Instead of using fear or shame, which would likely not motivate her, we start with curiosity. This involves asking open-ended questions to understand the root of the issue.

Letting the employee lead means allowing them to identify and propose solutions. People often know where things are going wrong and how to fix them.

The third cornerstone, coaching the whole person, recognizes that personal life affects work life. By acknowledging and addressing personal challenges, we can enhance engagement.

In a conversation between Christy and her manager Arnold, we see these principles in action. Arnold's curiosity and openness create a safe space for

Christy to share her challenges and ideas for improvement. He doesn't dictate, threaten, or dismiss her personal life. So, remember to be curious, let your employees take the lead, and coach the whole person to foster effective coaching relationships.

Three types of coaching conversations

Your coaching conversations are closely tied to achieving goals and typically follow a distinct pattern: clarity, implementation, and reflection.

Clarity conversations, often at the beginning, involve reviewing accomplishments, identifying strengths, and understanding what motivates and what people want to learn and be known for. In a conversation between Christy and Arnold, you can see the importance of asking open-ended questions to delve deeper into these aspects.

Implementation conversations focus on translating self-awareness and clarity into goals and responsibilities. Arnold and Christy discuss how to improve Christy's delegation skills by asking probing questions and setting specific action steps.

Reflection conversations create a pause to assess progress, acknowledge achievements, and potentially celebrate. Christy's progress with delegation is highlighted in a conversation with Arnold.

While these are shown as distinct conversations, they often intertwine as your employees work toward their goals or tackle challenges. A useful tip is to wait before giving direction, asking yourself, "Why am I talking?" This conserves your energy and gives your employees autonomy and a sense of accomplishment.

Asking powerful questions

Powerful questions are essential tools in coaching. They are open-ended and usually start with words like who, what, when, where, why, and how. These questions are valuable for helping your team gain clarity, self-awareness, explore options, and discover new perspectives. They encourage individuals to develop their own ideas and solutions. Closed-ended questions, like "Do you like your new office?" or "Are you enjoying your work with Mary?" only allow for simple yes or no answers and don't foster meaningful conversation or self-awareness. By reframing closed-ended questions into open-ended ones, such as "What do you think about your new office?" or "How are things working with

Mary?" you can encourage deeper thought and gather more insightful information.

Here are some powerful questions for various stages of coaching:

1. Starting a coaching conversation:

   - What have been your wins and challenges since our last discussion?

   - What would you like to focus on today?

2. Getting to the core of an issue or challenge:

   - What appears to be the primary obstacle?

   - What's preventing you from making progress?

   - What are your desired outcomes?

3. Exploring new perspectives:

   - If a similar situation arises again, what approach might you take?

   - Can you think of an alternative viewpoint?

   - What are all the potential solutions?

4. Planning and taking action:

   - How could you enhance the situation?

   - What's your strategy or game plan?

   - What are the next steps, and when do you plan to complete them?

Consider these questions as a helpful reference until you become more skilled as a coach. To improve your questioning technique, when you're tempted to offer advice or criticism, pause and begin your question with "what" or "how." This straightforward power tip will accelerate your coaching proficiency.

Increasing your listening skills

Coaching demands a unique form of listening. Throughout your education, you were trained to provide the correct answers, which is why, as a manager, you might feel compelled to offer direction and decisiveness. While these skills are valuable, coaching requires setting aside preconceived notions, avoiding interjecting your perspective, and listening differently.

For instance, imagine you have a team member facing time management and email overload challenges. You might think the solution is straightforward, instructing them to allocate focused time for cleanup. However, this external approach only provides a temporary fix and doesn't empower or involve the employee. There might be underlying issues left unexplored. Instead of listening followed by giving direction, you should aim to find the next appropriate question. Your goal is to help your team members source their own answers.

Here are four strategies to enhance your listening skills:

1. Be fully present and concentrate on the other person, clearing your mind of distractions.

2. Minimize interruptions by closing your door, silencing alerts, and momentarily disconnecting.

3. Use verbal cues like "uh-huh" and "yes," along with body language like nodding and smiling to signal that you're listening.

4. Mirror what you've heard when clarification is needed. Phrases like "What I'm hearing is..." or "It sounds like you're saying..." can help bring clarity.

By combining effective listening with powerful questions, you can facilitate your team's problem-solving and self-discovery. Instead of immediately providing solutions, ask open-ended questions like, "What's causing the logjam, and how can I help?" and allow the silence for reflection. Remember, the goal is to listen to discover the next appropriate question.

Challenging your people for growth

When should you challenge the individuals, you're coaching? There are a few key indicators. If a high-potential employee seems disengaged or uninterested, it's time to provide a challenge, such as a new opportunity or increased visibility, aligning with their talents. If someone consistently struggles to achieve a goal, it might be a should rather than a true goal. In such cases, it is essential to uncover what they genuinely desire and need and adjust or discard the goal accordingly. Resistance or procrastination may also indicate fear, and you can help individuals confront their fears by exploring potential outcomes or taking a small step forward.

Challenges should consider three aspects:

1. Alignment with personal and professional aspirations.

2. Appropriateness in terms of size and timing.

3. Acceptance by the individual for the challenge to be effective.

In a coaching conversation with Christy, her boss Arnold encouraged her to take on a challenge related to her goal of becoming a better delegator. Arnold suggested that Christy teach what she had learned to her team, even though it initially seemed overwhelming. Arnold kept Christy's aspirations in focus and helped her realize that her fear was holding her back from getting what she wanted. Christy ultimately accepted the challenge, leading to a significant breakthrough.

Challenging your employees can be complex, but it is essential to keep their aspirations at the forefront and find the right fit challenge that aligns with their goals and growth. In some cases, additional brainstorming may be required to identify the most appropriate challenge.

Brainstorming to build momentum

The initial three coaching practices – asking questions, listening, and challenging – generally lead to identifying next steps. However, when an employee is unsure about a solution and needs guidance on what actions to take, brainstorming can help uncover multiple solutions and potential courses of action. Before effective brainstorming, it's often necessary to create clarity by addressing three key questions: What do you want? What obstacles are in the way? What's the real issue?

For example, I worked with a Customer Success VP responsible for improving her company's client onboarding process. She faced a challenge in getting engineering and marketing to collaborate. Her goal was a more efficient collaboration that would reduce decision-making bottlenecks and better meet client needs, ultimately increasing retention and profits. Brainstorming helped her move from the "what" to the "how."

To facilitate brainstorming effectively, I recommend using two types of questions: "generators" and "deciders." Generators are meant to generate numerous ideas, and they include questions like: What have you tried already? What aspects of the problem have you not explored? What's missing that should be happening? What's your vision if everything goes as planned? Additionally, What's another option? and What else?

On the other hand, deciders help individuals pinpoint the right actions, and they involve questions like: What is the smallest or easiest step to take right now? What action would accelerate progress? What single move would set everything else in motion?

A crucial power tip is to maintain your commitment. If the next steps involve your approval for resource access or training, it's essential to follow through and keep your word.

Managing accountability

Accountability is an essential component of coaching, where employees transform the "what" into the "how." It encompasses three elements: the specific action the employee agrees to take, the timeline for doing it, and how you will confirm their achievement. Between making an agreement, taking action, and reporting results, there may be various challenges and opportunities for learning. Some agreements are straightforward, like scheduling a meeting and reporting its outcomes, while others are more complex, such as organizing workshops or training sessions. For lengthy agreements, it's advisable to help employees set milestones and clarify how and when they'll communicate their progress.

It's crucial to remember that failure is part of the learning process. Missed deadlines, errors, and procrastination are all part of the journey, and as a manager, it's vital to provide support rather than belittle your employees when they encounter setbacks.

In a scenario involving Christy, a team lead, and her manager, Arnold, Christy is dealing with challenges in implementing new workflow systems. Arnold facilitates the conversation, guiding Christy to explore possible solutions and create accountabilities. The focus is on helping her navigate through the challenges and stay accountable to her goals despite the complexities of the process.

Coaching and Developing Employees

Future-focused feedback comprises three phases: understanding what happened, seeking improvement for the future, and drawing lessons for the future. Unlike traditional performance feedback, which often dwells on past mistakes and promotes defensiveness, future-focused feedback focuses on possibilities and growth. It encourages individuals to express their feelings and describe what occurred. When faced with a situation like a missed deadline or a botched project, you can initiate future-focused feedback as follows:

1. Express your disappointment and ask, "What happened?" This phase allows employees to share their perspective without blame.

2. Collaboratively explore solutions with questions like, "How can we turn things around?" Emphasize teamwork and shared responsibility.

3. Reflect on how to avoid similar situations in the future by asking, "What can we do to prevent this from happening again?" This phase promotes learning and forward-thinking.

Adopting future-focused feedback may require practice if you tend to default to criticism and judgment. Use the power tip of pausing and gathering your thoughts to ensure a constructive conversation. This feedback approach maintains trust, sustains momentum, and keeps everyone focused on achieving common goals. It is the type of feedback that emanates from leadership and inspires leadership.

The GROW model

One of the simplest coaching frameworks, ideal for initiating your coaching relationship, is the GROW Model. GROW stands for Goals, Realities, Options, and Way Forward.

Goals represent the specific outcomes your employees wish to achieve. They should be clear and well-defined. Realities are all about the current situation and challenges related to the goal. Options involve exploring various possibilities to make progress, while Way Forward focuses on choosing the next steps and adding accountability through timing or due dates.

To help you transition from giving directives to coaching, here are some introductory open-ended questions for each aspect of the GROW Model.

For Goals:

- Where do you aspire to grow in your role or career?

- What is it that you want to be recognized for?

For Realities:

- What progress have you made toward your goals?

- What obstacles are hindering your progress?

For Options:

- What strategies have you already attempted?

- What possibilities can you think of?

- Who might assist you?

- What's the most significant step you can take now, or what's the first small step?

For the Way Forward:

- What are your planned next steps?

- What are you committing to, and by when?

- How will we confirm your progress?

These final two questions are essential, not only for accountability but also for maintaining a consistent coaching process. The GROW Model is an excellent starting point for your coaching relationship.

The ORID framework

The ORID framework is a method that involves asking questions in stages. ORID stands for Objective, Reflective, Interpretive, and Decisional. This framework aligns with behavioral science, facilitating the learning and information processing processes, as well as decision-making influenced by both logic and emotion. You can apply the ORID framework in one-on-one sessions and as a valuable tool for meetings and facilitation.

1. Objective Questions - Focus on gathering facts and data:

- What is the challenge in one sentence?

- What happened in one minute or less?

2. Reflective Questions - Elicit feelings and thoughts about the facts:

   - What are your thoughts and feelings about what just happened?

   - What was the impact on you and others?

3. Interpretive Questions - Explore meaning, assumptions, and implications:

   - What do you make of it?

   - What are you learning from this experience?

   - What other perspectives might be valuable?

   - And what else?

4. Decisional Questions - Address priorities and next steps:

   - Where do we go from here?

   - What are the next steps?

   - What are you committing to?

The ORID framework is adaptable and effective, whether you have a full hour or just a brief 10-minute conversation. It's a reliable structure that encourages productive discussions and decision-making.

The Clarity Questionnaire

I have another valuable tool for your team: the Clarity Questionnaire. It helps individuals identify their values, strengths, capacities, and future learning needs. The Clarity Questionnaire is a foundational tool for manager-coaches looking to develop their team's depth.

The questionnaire guides individuals to reflect deeply on key aspects of their work and life. It starts by assessing the current state with questions such as, "What topics do you enjoy learning and discussing? What are you passionate about to the point of doing it for free? What are your reliable strengths recognized by friends and colleagues?" These responses reveal values, strengths, skills, and recurring themes.

The second set of questions focuses on accomplishments and impact, not only in the present role but also in previous positions. Questions include, "What have you achieved recently? What about in the past year? What results have you produced over the last five years?" These questions help quantify impact and identify recurring strengths, skills, and competencies.

The third set of questions delves into competencies that individuals want to prioritize, especially those in high demand in the market or industry. They address what competencies enable value creation, emerging opportunities, and the top 10 competencies in high demand. Individuals must assess if they possess or can develop these competencies and support their predictions with research.

Finally, after answering the previous questions, individuals can connect the dots and take action. Questions include, "How does your current role align with your desired reputation? What options can move you closer to your goals? What's the fastest option?" By the end, this questionnaire equips individuals to draft their unique value proposition and articulate their value effectively.

While this questionnaire may initially require an investment of time to review responses, it empowers individuals to drive their personal and professional development. By completing this task, they gain clarity on their value, ultimately leading to a more recognized and respected team.

The influence interview

The valuable Influence Interview exercise seeking feedback from people who know you well, such as family, friends, and colleagues. The goal is to understand how they perceive your strengths and areas for improvement. The Influence Interview may reveal unexpected insights. For example, one client who believed she was overly opinionated and talkative in meetings discovered the opposite was true; colleagues wanted her to speak up more.

Here is how it works: Your employees should create a list of people to interview via email, typically around five to seven individuals. They will ask two sets of questions focusing on strengths and reality checks. The strengths questions include inquiries like, "What are my greatest strengths? What skills do I consistently bring to the table? Which strengths and skills have been most valuable to you?" The reality check questions involve exploring areas of struggle, self-sabotage, and opportunities for improvement. For instance, "Where do you see me facing challenges? How do I hinder myself? What immediate steps could I take to enhance my performance? What would you do in my shoes?"

To ensure a straightforward process, a power tip is to reassure the recipients in the email that they won't need to provide justifications or defenses and only need to respond with two words: "Thank you."

While the Influence Interview may initially seem daunting, it can be transformational in helping individuals gain a deeper understanding of themselves and their impact on others. This task can also provide clarity on where to focus coaching efforts. So, encourage your employees to be brave and try the Influence Interview. The hope is that they will find the results pleasantly surprising.

Designing stretch opportunities

Daniel Pink's book "Drive" emphasizes that people are often more motivated by having control over their lives than by financial incentives. They want to feel valued and that their contributions matter. These individuals have a thirst for learning and applying what they have learned.

1. Learning and Education: Begin your coaching journey by inquiring about your employees' educational aspirations and see how you can support them. Informal options include workshops, conferences, certifications, and online courses. For more formal education, some companies offer undergraduate or advanced degrees like an MBA as employee benefits. A power tip here is to identify early, using the clarity questionnaire, your team members' learning interests and encourage them to explore available internal and external resources. It's crucial to establish a timeline for achieving their learning goals and protect that timeline from being overwhelmed by emergencies.

2. Mentoring: Unlike coaching, mentoring involves providing guidance and direction to a mentee, often a junior-level employee aspiring to reach the mentor's position. Mentors typically share their expertise and experiences voluntarily. To offer this stretch opportunity, think about your employees' goals and ambitions and connect them with leaders both within and outside the organization who can guide and inspire them.

3. Sponsorship: If you have a high-performing team member seeking new opportunities and greater visibility, consider sponsoring them. This means

actively supporting and advocating for your employees, using your reputation to make introductions and open doors to help them advance in their careers.

4. Teach Others: An excellent way to solidify your understanding of the coaching practices you've learned in this course is to teach others. Share your coaching knowledge and practices with the individuals you plan to coach. Be transparent about your process. Over time, coaching can become a part of your team's culture, enhancing results, your visibility, and your leadership potential.

Now, after all your efforts to become a great manager-coach, what do you do when some people are resistant to the idea of coaching?

Working through resistance

Employee development coaching is centered on self-reflection and growth, which often involves change – a challenging process for some individuals. When your team members take on new projects or stretch assignments, resistance or pushback is quite normal. It is essential to recognize that not everyone you manage may be willing or ready to be coached, and not everyone is suitable for coaching.

1. Some individuals lack the experience and skills for self-directed learning, requiring substantial guidance and mentorship.

2. Others may not possess the emotional capability for the deeper self-reflective work that coaching entails.

3. A few highly self-directed and competent individuals might not see the value in coaching, beyond quick check-ins.

Rather than making coaching mandatory for all employees, it's advisable to start with those who are willing and ready. This approach allows the benefits of coaching to naturally permeate the team. In essence, meet people where they are in their developmental journey.

As you gain expertise in coaching, you can discreetly incorporate coaching principles, such as using the ORID framework and open-ended questions, without drawing attention to the coaching process.

Even among coachable individuals, an initial objection often revolves around the question, "What am I doing wrong?" For high-achievers, assure them that coaching is not a corrective measure but a means to expedite their growth and advancement. For those who may be less experienced or underperforming, express your intention to help them leverage their strengths and achieve success.

When coaching your employees, you might encounter issues like tardiness, missed meetings, deadlines, or low participation. Here are some guidelines to address such challenges:

1. Don't take these issues personally; focus on the problem rather than the person.

2. Use open-ended questions to address objections or issues. Convert any criticisms into open-ended inquiries.

3. Allow people to vent without interruption or immediate feedback. Sometimes, individuals need to express their feelings or frustrations.

4. Acknowledge what's happening but avoid commiserating. Stay empathetic and maintain a focus on their larger goals, enabling them to find their way forward.

Finally, if an employee displays disengagement through body language (e.g., folded arms or minimal eye contact), it is crucial to recognize this geography. You can mirror their posture or movement and inquire about the meaning behind these behaviors. With persistence and empathy, you can overcome resistance and keep the coaching process on track.

Coaching remotely

In the evolving world of remote work, physical and psychological challenges arise due to less in-person interaction. However, since remote work is becoming the norm, let's focus on the advantages and best practices of remote coaching.

Geography of Coaching:

1. Observation: When using video, you can still observe body language, tone, facial expressions, and even the unspoken moments, similar to in-person coaching.

2. Privacy: While you cannot physically close a door, you can silence distractions, use hearing devices, and give your full attention to your employees.

3. Perspective Shifting: Encourage employees to change their physical location while coaching to gain a fresh perspective.

4. Professional Focus: Coaching remotely, through phone or video chat, eliminates physical distractions and enhances your ability to focus on your client's experience.

Structure of Remote Conversations:

1. Get Connected: Start with a brief personal conversation, showing interest in your employees' lives and sharing about your own.

2. Specify Time: Clarify the duration of the conversation.

3. Address Work-Related Matters: Quickly handle any time-sensitive work topics at the beginning.

4. Discuss Wins and Challenges: Ask about recent accomplishments and challenges since your last meeting. Then, inquire about their focus for the current session.

5. End with Action: Determine the next steps and what your employee will be accountable for before the next meeting.

It is important to note that you can establish a strong connection even in audio-only conversations with practice. Offering flexibility, such as the choice between video and audio calls, can be beneficial. Experiment with these geography and structure techniques to enhance your coaching effectiveness and foster engagement in a remote work environment.

Chapter 2 Coach Your Team to Learn, Stretch, and Grow

Is your team working to its full potential?

Do you have employees who seem content with mediocrity, just doing their job? Or do you have those who are constantly seeking new and improved ways to work, driven by curiosity and a thirst for challenges? As a leader, you can nurture their hunger for growth and improvement by offering appropriate challenges and opportunities. It is essential not to overburden them with more work as a reward for their performance. Instead, engage in conversations to understand their preferences and areas for development. By fostering a culture of internal mobility and development, you can keep employees motivated and engaged, helping them realize their full potential.

Make learning opportunities accessible

In organizations, it is common to send below-average employees to courses and workshops to help them meet performance standards. However, we often overlook those employees who are eager to learn new skills or enhance existing ones. They may hesitate to request advanced learning opportunities, fearing they are diverting resources or exposing their weaknesses. But, in reality, these employees are driven by a desire to grow and excel. As a manager, you can play a crucial role in nurturing their potential.

Start by involving them in the process. Ask what skills they wish to acquire or improve, emphasizing the value of lifelong learning. Encourage them to share their preferred learning format, whether it is interactive classes, self-paced reading, online modules, or mentorship. It is important to remember that not all learning requires a formal degree or certification. A modest learning budget can yield significant results. Since most employees will not proactively seek out these opportunities, take the initiative to inquire about their learning preferences and actively involve them in planning their educational journey. This approach can empower them to unlock their potential.

Use learning and development plans

Continuous learning is essential throughout one's career, and it is often workplace learning that truly matters. Consider the case of John Jarvis, who rose through the ranks to become the director of the National Park Service, responsible for vast territories, budgets, and personnel. Jarvis's approach to learning holds valuable lessons. He consistently identified the skills he needed to improve and sought relevant classes and workshops, demonstrating a dynamic approach to skill development.

For your team members, the same principles apply. Encourage them to identify skills or processes requiring enhancement and then look for suitable classes, workshops, or informal learning opportunities. These don't necessitate complete degrees; focused skill-sharpening courses are available through local colleges or online learning platforms. Additionally, consider learning from peers and fellow professionals. Networking, sharing experiences, and observing experts can provide valuable insights and solutions. Facilitate connections between team members and experts within your organization and promote collaborative learning within your sector.

Remember that learning opportunities abound. Create a clear plan for your team members, specifying the skills or processes they need to learn, identifying relevant learning opportunities, setting timelines, and establishing accountability. Goals are only realized through well-structured plans, and your guidance and accountability will enable your team to achieve their objectives.

Why managers should help their employees learn

If your employees can operate the latest smartphones, they can certainly learn new skills. The pace of learning may vary, but the opportunities exist. As a manager, you can help employees expand their skill set in various ways. Research indicates that employees are eager to learn and adapt.

This research underscores the likelihood that your team members want to learn new skills. Once you identify the skills they need to develop, explore available avenues. Consult your organization's learning and development department (L&D) for internal offerings. Determine who covers the costs; check if the company provides upskilling benefits. Communicate this benefit to employees and emphasize its value.

Investing in upskilling your employees enhances efficiency, innovation, and the bottom line. Implementing these steps can significantly impact your team's upskilling, internal mobility, and loyalty to the organization.

Anticipate the learning needs of your employees

We have two eyes and two ears but only one mouth, implying we should observe and listen twice as much as we speak. Watching others can be highly informative. As a manager, you can apply this principle to anticipate your team's needs and show your interest in their success. To do so, look for clues in their preferences and struggles. Identify what they enjoy and where there are gaps or sources of stress. Observe their reactions, finding moments that light up their faces with enthusiasm. By noticing and helping your team address their challenges proactively, you will become known as a caring manager who fosters growth, even before they voice their needs.

Communities of practice

Encourage your employees to find or create communities, whether within the company, industry, or region. The common thread can be anything, and communication can happen through tools like Listserv, Facebook groups, Slack channels, or WhatsApp. Communities of practice make work less isolating, enhance independence, and offer opportunities and ideas. You can assist your employees in finding or forming these communities and empower them to share the same with others, fostering a network of support and collaboration.

The benefits of stretch assignments

Do you recall the first time you used new software, like PowerPoint or Zoom? It felt unfamiliar at the start, but as you got comfortable, you began exploring its features. To foster your team's growth, you cannot have them stuck in routine tasks; they will get bored and complacent. Encourage them to step out of their comfort zones through stretch assignments, which combine greater responsibility with learning a new skill. A Korn Ferry study found that stretch assignments are the most effective way to develop leadership skills. Determine what skills your employees need to improve, be it technical, strategic, or interpersonal. Tailor stretch assignments to these skill areas; for example, let them make a crucial presentation to a VIP client or lead the implementation of a new process. The benefits include skill development, exposure to new experiences, and a boost in their self-confidence.

For organizations, stretch assignments are a cost-effective tool for employee development and succession planning. However, as a manager, balance the level of challenge and support, ensure the assignments are suitable for each team member's rank, ability, and interests, and offer scaffolding to ease their transition into new tasks. Regular check-ins are essential to gauge their progress and address any difficulties they encounter. By providing the right blend of support and challenge, you can create a continuously growing and innovative team through stretch assignments, igniting their enthusiasm to try something new.

When to let team members "just do it"

Reading, watching videos, and consulting experts are excellent initial steps to gain foundational knowledge. However, true understanding and skill come from hands-on experience. This is known as experiential learning. It allows you to try things, learn through trial and error, and feel the adrenaline that accompanies success or potential failure. Everyone has their unique way of learning, and learning through experience requires diving in, taking action, and getting hands-on. So, are you prepared to let your team learn by doing?

Coach your team to dream big

The phrase "We've always done it that way" is use to defend the status quo, I can't help but think of Blockbuster, the video rental store. While Netflix introduced a new way of mailing and streaming movies to your home, Blockbuster clung to its brick-and-mortar store model. They could not see the changing landscape and failed to explore new needs and models. Their resistance to change ultimately led to Blockbuster's demise. We all desire innovation and want to create something new, but it is daunting to get started. It seems like a massive task, and people often feel stuck. Instead of inventing entirely new concepts, innovation can come from using old ideas in new ways. Taxis and hotels were not new, but changing the model brought us Uber and Airbnb. As a manager, when your team is hesitant to start from scratch, encourage them to consider these questions. They can help your team think about old problems in new ways:

1. How can we make a product or process more efficient?

2. Create an empathy map that lists what people say, do, think, and feel about a specific product or process to identify the real problem.

3. Use mind mapping to generate multiple ideas around a single topic.

4. Explore who we might be overlooking in the process.

These questions will inspire your team to think bigger and find unconventional solutions to age-old challenges.

Help your team think differently

I use a process called Design Thinking developed by IDEO, a company known for designing products like the Apple mouse and dental floss dispensers. Their approach encourages you to reconsider your assumptions by examining a problem from multiple angles, always starting with the user at the center.

IDEO stands out by assembling diverse teams of engineers, psychologists, marketing experts, and behavioral scientists from various generations. This diversity of perspectives leads to fresh insights and innovative thinking. Diverse teams make quicker decisions, foster creativity, and boost employee engagement.

As a manager, you can promote different thinking in your team by ensuring they have diverse backgrounds and experiences. Encourage hiring individuals with unique skills and experiences. When working on projects, consider adding members from different divisions or departments to bring fresh perspectives. For example, including a marketer in an accounting team can offer new insights.

This approach not only solves problems more effectively but also enhances your team's problem-solving and innovation skills. With diverse teams, creating something new or tackling challenges becomes an exciting creative endeavor. So, how will you diversify your team?

Support struggling employees

Sometimes, we tend to overcomplicate and overthink things. A guiding hand and a gentle nudge in the right direction can make all the difference. As a manager, if you notice a team member overly fixated on the end goal and missing the journey, consider these steps: slow things down, emphasize the project's purpose, break it into manageable parts, provide support when they face difficulties, and encourage them to take a break or shift focus if needed. Openly discuss the project's significance and how their role contributes to the big picture. By making tasks more manageable, you demonstrate that your team can achieve more than they thought possible.

The power of mentors

Research unequivocally supports the value of mentorship, showing that mentored individuals earn more, perform better, enjoy their careers, experience fewer burnout cases, and secure more raises and promotions.

As a manager, you can assist by recommending potential mentors to your mentee, helping fill gaps in their knowledge and providing fresh perspectives. Consider individuals both within and outside your industry, spanning different seniority levels. Facilitate introductions with specific context, explaining why you believe the connection is beneficial. This approach ensures clarity and focuses on the mentee's needs.

If you believe your mentee would benefit from acquiring or advancing specific skills, engage in a development conversation. Discuss options such as classes or conferences, expressing your belief in their potential and offering sponsorship. This not only fosters growth but also enhances retention.

The role of sponsors

We have all heard about groups of colleagues who socialize outside of work and seem to get chosen for prime assignments and promotions. What sets them apart? People prefer working with those they know, like, and trust. Those who socialize get to know each other on a personal level, building camaraderie. If someone is not included, it is not because they are not liked; they simply are not known personally.

While promotions are not always purely merit-based, you can influence change. Help your direct reports stand out for choice assignments and promotions by discussing their accomplishments in their absence. Promote their hard work and recent achievements, recommend them for special opportunities and awards, and create visibility for them. Celebrate their successes on social media to boost their morale. When positions open up, encourage them to apply and advocate for them with hiring managers. Your influence can create substantial opportunities, so leverage it positively.

The coaching manager

Coaches are not exclusive to top athletes or CEOs. You can apply key coaching skills to help your team members grow. Start with the Grow model, which stands for Goal, Reality, Opportunities (or Obstacles), and Will:

1. Goal: Help your team members define both short and long-term goals, articulating what they want to achieve in one, three, and five years.

2. Reality: Evaluate the current situation. Make sure their goals align with their abilities and circumstances.

3. Opportunities/Obstacles: Identify what options and strengths they can leverage, as well as any roadblocks they might face.

4. Will: Develop a plan with clear steps and hold them accountable to achieve their goals. Use regular check-in meetings and external resources as needed.

The first step is helping your team members clarify their goals. Once they have a goal in mind, you can work together to create a practical plan for them to achieve it. If you are not the right coach for them, consider finding one within or outside your organization.

Stretch like a rubberband

Consider each team member as a rubber band; once stretched, they will not return to their original form. Equipped with the tools to push people out of their comfort zones and promote growth, you are on your way to building an exceptional team. You will be recognized for bringing out the best in people.

Chapter 3 Coaching Your Team in a Dynamic Workplace

Strengths-based coaching

What do Steve Jobs, Serena Williams, and Sir Elton John have in common? Peak performance? Absolutely, but more than that, they excel at work by prioritizing their strengths. High performers don't ignore their development areas, but if you want to join their ranks, start by identifying, nurturing, and growing your signature strengths. As a manager, you can create a high-performing, productive, and motivated team through strengths-based coaching. Here's how:

1. Gain buy-in: Have open discussions with your team members about the importance of focusing on strengths to enhance performance, productivity, and motivation.

2. Identify signature strengths: Collaboratively select the top three natural strengths of each team member and focus on their development in coaching conversations.

3. Balance strengths and development: Allocate approximately 70% of coaching time to signature strengths, 20% to building new potential strengths, and 10% to enhancing development areas.

4. Monitor progress: Track the impact of using strengths on performance, productivity, motivation, and relationships during coaching sessions. Focus on achievements and tangible outcomes.

With strengths-based coaching, you empower your team members to be authentic, using their strengths to meet targets and address challenges in ways that align with their personality and abilities. Set the destination but let them choose their unique journey.

GROW coaching model

As a busy manager, it is essential to use simple and effective coaching tools, especially for large teams. The GROW Model is a streamlined method to empower your team members to take ownership of their skill development.

1. Goal: Collaboratively identify stretching yet achievable goals. Ask questions like: What do you aim to achieve? How does it fit into the bigger picture? What smaller steps can you take this week or month?

2. Reality: Understand the current situation and potential barriers. Encourage your team member to draw on their strengths. Questions like: What is the current situation? What barriers might arise? How can your qualities and available resources help you overcome obstacles?

3. Options: Explore various ways to reach the goal. Let your team member lead the conversation, adding ideas if needed. Questions like: What are the options for achieving your goal? How might others approach it? What's the most appealing approach?

4. Will: Agree on specific actions and ensure accountability. Questions like: What actions will you take? How will you track progress and measure success? How committed are you to taking action?

If action steps are challenging, revisit the options part until your team member identifies an approach, they are comfortable with. Put this coaching technique into practice to help your team achieve tangible goals.

Feedback coaching tool

Coaching primarily looks toward the future and potential achievements. However, it is crucial to leverage past data, promote self-reflection, and gather feedback to enhance future effectiveness. In feedback coaching, concentrate on three key aspects:

1. Personal Reflection: Encourage regular self-reflection to inform future strategies. Simple questions like "What have you done well recently?" and "How can you improve in the future?" aid this process.

2. Feedback from Others: Emphasize informal feedback collection. Encourage your team member to ask, "What could I do even better?" This positive, future-focused question makes it easier for others to provide input.

3. Manager Feedback: Offer your feedback as part of the coaching process, focusing on areas for improvement. Concentrate on the "even-better-if" approach to guide your team member's future strategy.

By addressing all three feedback areas, you can collaboratively use feedback to feed forward and help your team achieve future goals effectively.

Coaching in a complex matrixed organization

Coaching within a complex matrix organization demands specific skills. These companies, often large and multinational, have dual reporting structures, creating role ambiguities and communication challenges. Coaching team members who report to others can be tricky, here are some key coaching strategies:

1. Focus on Personal Development: Enhance your coaching skills to navigate this unique environment effectively.

2. Build Trust: Prioritize trust-building to show genuine concern for your team members, helping them navigate complexities and create opportunities.

3. Shift Perspectives: Understand your coaches' viewpoints, listening without making assumptions, and adapting your support accordingly.

4. Clarify Confidentiality: While you may not share everything, maintain confidentiality in your coaching conversations to build trust.

5. Acknowledge Complexities: Recognize that your opinion may not always take precedence, openly addressing the need for your team members to consider different views and expectations.

6. Foster a Collaborative Learning Style: Use coaching sessions to learn from your coaches, ask questions, and collaborate with other managers who influence your team, building your network and relationships.

7. Stay Open-Minded: Focus on understanding your team member's role, allowing you to provide effective support and guidance.

Coaching in a virtual world

The pandemic accelerated the shift towards virtual working. To effectively coach your team in this environment, consider the following tips:

1. Understand Working Preferences: Learn your team members' preferences regarding work-life balance and work environment. Are they boundary-driven or prefer a blended approach? Acknowledge any personal constraints affecting their choices.

2. Role Modeling: Share your own experiences with virtual work, managing well-being, and promoting mental health. Discuss the pros and cons to help them create an effective schedule.

3. Discuss Performance and Outcomes: Address the challenges of remote work, such as reduced visibility and connection. Explore ways to champion your team members, make their achievements visible, and facilitate networking opportunities.

4. Manage Logistics: Decide on the logistics of coaching sessions, including the mode (video or phone) and frequency. Maintain consistency in your virtual meetings to prevent them from slipping.

5. Problem-Solving: Collaboratively address challenges in the virtual working arrangement. Encourage your coaches to lead the problem-solving process, finding solutions that benefit all stakeholders.

Coaching in a virtual work environment demands adaptability, and it is a crucial skill as virtual and flexible work arrangements are set to become more common in the future.

Coaching across cultures

Coaching people from diverse cultures, whether in a large multinational or a small startup, is crucial for modern managers. To excel at coaching across cultures, consider these key tips:

1. Focus on Similarities, Not Differences: Don't get caught up in stereotypes about how people from different regions communicate or behave. Treat individuals as unique, with distinct personalities and needs. Adapt your coaching to their specific responses.

2. Be Sensitive to Cultural Norms: Avoid relying on fixed lists of cultural differences; instead, cultivate adaptability in your coaching style. Approach each

coaching session with a growth mindset and a willingness to learn. Test different approaches, seek feedback, and adapt your style accordingly.

3. Agree on a Test Approach: Engage in open conversations with coaches to understand their preferences and expectations. Find a middle ground and regularly review what's working and what isn't. Encourage coaches to lead the conversation, avoiding a one-size-fits-all approach.

By combining curiosity, adaptability, continuous learning, and feedback, you can become an effective cross-cultural coach as a manager.

Coaching across generations

Today's workplace encompasses up to five generations: Traditionalists, Baby Boomers, Generation X, Millennials (Generation Y), and Generation Z (Digital Natives). These generational differences are influenced by life stages and socioeconomic factors. As a manager, it is vital to adapt your coaching style to each team member. Here are key tips:

1. Understand Strengths and Motivations: Get to know the unique strengths and motivations of your team members. Ask about what drives them and the challenges they typically encounter.

2. Embrace Reverse Coaching: Remember that every team member has valuable insights. Learn from their perspectives, whether it's a new graduate introducing new technology or an experienced colleague shaping your strategies.

3. Manage Coaching Expectations: Recognize that not everyone will respond to the same coaching style. Adapt your approach to suit each individual, whether it's a deep coaching session or a brief catch-up.

In today's diverse workplace, where multiple generations coexist, your ability to tailor your coaching strategies will be a valuable asset throughout your managerial career.

Coaching in a purpose-driven workplace

As a manager, this opens up the potential for untapped motivation in your team, with members seeking to work with a sense of purpose. You can leverage coaching to help your team work meaningfully, enhance productivity, and increase engagement.

Here are the steps you can take:

1. Understand Motivations: Collaborate with your team members to explore what motivates them. Discover their internal and external drivers, including personal fulfillment, helping others, recognition, and financial incentives. If they express a need for meaning, move on to the next step.

2. Align with Purpose: Help your team members connect their roles to the organization's purpose and goals. Encourage them to see how their work contributes to the broader mission.

3. Recognize and Contribute: Recognize and value the contributions of those seeking purpose within your team. Acknowledging their efforts in line with your team's mission will help cultivate a sense of purpose. Work with them to discover how they can infuse purpose into their tasks, but ensure this is a genuine and voluntary pursuit.

4. Ask the Right Question: When helping team members identify their purpose becomes challenging, ask a powerful question: "If money were no object, and you could do something meaningful every day, what would it be?"

By following these coaching steps, you can help your team members find meaning and purpose in their work.

Coaching through change

In today's ever-evolving workplace, change is inevitable and it is happening faster than ever before. Technological advancements, competition, and economic shifts are the driving forces behind this rapid transformation. As a manager, understanding how people respond to change is valuable, but it is also important not to get too fixated on specific stages of change, as these can vary widely from person to person. Instead, I recommend focusing on practical coaching tools to help your team navigate continuous change and uncertainty while maintaining their productivity and performance.

During coaching sessions, concentrate on three key areas to empower your team members in times of change:

1. Encourage Flexibility: Given the constantly changing nature of work, adaptability is a vital skill. Some individuals are naturally more flexible in their thinking and ability to handle change, but everyone will need to develop this skill further. Challenge your team members to explore different perspectives by

asking questions like, "How else can we look at this situation?" and "How might someone else react in this context?" The goal is to help them question their own assumptions and realize there are multiple ways to perceive and respond to a situation.

2. Identify Opportunities: Despite the discomfort change may bring, it also opens doors to opportunities. Discuss potential positive outcomes in changing situations. Consider pairing team members with those who thrive in change so they can foster a culture of optimism and seize opportunities together.

3. Foster Resilience: Empower your team members to cope effectively with change, see obstacles as chances for growth, and focus on actionable steps to excel in their current environment. Start by discussing how ambiguity can be exciting and identify actions they can take to regain a sense of control. Offer suggestions if needed but encourage them to take the lead in these coaching sessions.

While you may have encountered or even experienced the stages of the change curve, remember that each team member is unique, and their response to change is influenced by their personality and personal circumstances. By letting them take the lead in coaching sessions, you can create a coaching environment that suits their individual needs, strengthening your relationship in the process.

Coaching for creativity and innovation

Whether your work involves organizing trade shows or staying ahead of industry trends for a competitive edge, one critical area of focus is creativity and innovation. Creativity is a highly sought-after skill in today's business world, and it's the first step toward innovation. As a manager, how can you coach your team to enhance their creative and innovative abilities?

First, embrace the idea of making mistakes. This applies to both your ability to accept your team's results, even if they fall short of your expectations, and helping your team members become comfortable with failure. Creativity involves generating novel ideas and exploring new paths that may not yield immediate success. You need to coach yourself to accept that errors are a natural part of the process. Encourage your team to focus on the creative process, such as brainstorming unique ideas, testing different approaches, and drawing inspiration from diverse sources. While it is essential to celebrate successful creative endeavors and analyze failures, the main focus of coaching conversations should be on the process of creativity itself.

Second, develop your skill in providing honest feedback. When creativity and innovation are priorities, you must be capable of delivering constructive yet challenging feedback. Instead of saying, "No, that will not work," try saying, "Yes, and maybe we could add another feature or align it with the sales team's focus." It is a positive approach to collaboration.

Finally, exemplify a growth mindset. Be open, honest, and vulnerable when you make a mistake, demonstrating how you use such situations for learning, growth, and ultimately, finding better solutions. This sets a powerful example for your team. In the realm of creativity and innovation, there is no straightforward path to success; it is the nature of these processes. It is sometimes challenging to be an effective coaching manager in this area because you may need to coach yourself to cope with the discomfort of unexpected outcomes before coaching your team members. Start by reflecting on your own responses to failure and create strategies to deal with these situations.

Building your coaching skills

Great coaches are not necessarily born with an inherent ability to coach effectively; these skills are developed and refined over time. Regardless of whether coaching feels natural or not, all coaches need to actively work on becoming better at it. Here are some key areas to focus on as you continue to enhance your coaching skills:

1. Improve your listening skills: When coaching, listen with the intent of understanding the other person's perspective, not just formulating your response. Take your time to respond after active listening.

2. Balance leading and exploring: In coaching, let your team member lead the conversation and explore their experiences, viewpoints, and goals. Sometimes, this means refraining from offering solutions, even when you think you have the perfect one.

3. Focus on guiding, not judging: Be aware of your potential bias as a manager with a vested interest in your team member's performance. Minimize judgment and concentrate on guiding your team member.

4. Learn the art of reframing: Help others reframe challenges by identifying opportunities within them. Encourage different perspectives and alternative ways of viewing obstacles while acknowledging the emotional impact of challenging situations.

5. Stay flexible and avoid assuming you have all the answers: Your perspective may provide valuable insights, but it doesn't necessarily mean you have the definitive solution. There are often multiple approaches to achieve positive results. Base feedback on observable facts and collaborate with your team member to fill in any information gaps.

6. Build trust: Establish boundaries for confidentiality, uphold your commitments, and practice honesty, even when it's difficult. Trust is crucial in coaching relationships.

As a coaching manager, your development is ongoing. Choose specific areas to focus on for enhancing your coaching skills, and consider working on them with your own coach. Remember that self-improvement as a coach is a continuous journey.

Chapter 4 Coaching Your Team to Think and Act Strategically

Using coaching to build strategic skills

If you want to enhance your team's strategic thinking and actions, you might be wondering if it is possible and how to go about it. Typically, we focus on creating roles and experiences that nurture strategic skills, like rotating team members to provide a broader business perspective, challenging them with new tasks, or involving them in strategic initiatives. While this approach is effective, we should also consider how our everyday management style impacts strategic thinking. Many busy managers tend to prioritize expedience, often resulting in a directive approach where they simply tell their team what to do. This approach offers quick solutions in the short term but fails to build the necessary strategic capability in the long run.

To foster strategic skills, it's beneficial to adopt a coaching style. Coaching encourages your team to think independently, so you should be curious about their decision-making processes, understand their perspectives, and provide tools instead of solutions. You have likely heard the saying, "Give a man a fish, and you feed him for a day; teach a man to fish, and you feed him for a lifetime." The same principle applies to coaching. By asking more questions, listening attentively, and teaching your team to experiment and reflect, you cultivate strategic skills that benefit their entire careers and make your role as a manager much smoother.

What does it mean to be strategic?

The term "strategic" is frequently used, but not everyone grasps how to put it into action. When you've told a team member to be more strategic, it is crucial to recognize that they may interpret this feedback differently. Some may think they need to participate in formal strategic planning, while others may perceive it as a need to improve their forward-thinking skills. To provide clearer guidance, we must define what it means to be strategic. Being strategic involves leading ourselves, our teams, and our organizations in a way that advances the organization's mission and goals, creating long-term advantages. This entails aligning our actions with our objectives, maintaining a future-oriented perspective, and focusing on meaningful matters at the department or company level. Strategic individuals possess various skills, such as a keen awareness of internal and external trends, the ability to anticipate issues and opportunities, a talent for prioritization, and effective communication to guide others toward new ideas. To enhance your development conversations, replace vague feedback with this more precise definition of being strategic in performance reviews and development plans.

A framework for thinking and acting strategically

To cultivate strategic skills in your team, emphasize two main competencies: strategic thinking and strategic behavior. Many team members understand the importance of strategic thinking, even if they struggle to practice it effectively. Strategic thinking involves the ability to connect pertinent information in novel and valuable ways, allowing them to detect early signs of opportunities or threats. To excel in this area, encourage curiosity and question-asking, as well as perspective-taking, to assess risks and consequences comprehensively.

However, strategic thinking alone is insufficient. To be recognized as strategic, your team must exhibit strategic behavior. This involves effective communication, time management aligned with priorities, and the willingness to take appropriate risks or challenge the status quo. By coaching your team in both strategic thinking and strategic behaviors, you equip them with the tools needed for both intellectual and interpersonal aspects of being strategic.

Mindset matters

Before embarking on coaching others, it is vital to acknowledge the importance of assessing your own beliefs and understanding how they might influence the coaching process and its outcomes. Your personal views and managerial experiences can either expand or constrain your team members' display of strategic behaviors. In essence, your mindset plays a significant role in this process.

To prepare for coaching, consider the following questions:

1. What are your beliefs regarding strategic work and who should be involved?

2. How have your past work experiences shaped your perception of strategic work and who is considered strategic?

3. How do you define strategic behavior?

It is essential to adopt a mindset that recognizes the value of developing everyone's strategic abilities, rather than restricting it to senior or specific team members. Individuals from various roles and levels can contribute to strategic thinking, and they should be nurtured accordingly. For example, customer-facing team members can offer insights into customer needs, while cross-functional team members can highlight how decisions impact different areas of the organization. New hires can bring fresh perspectives to strategic challenges.

Furthermore, assess how your existing beliefs may impact the coaching process. If you believe that strategic skills can only be honed through specific job experiences, you may miss opportunities for skill development in everyday interactions. If you view strategic work as something separate from day-to-day tasks, you might not approach coaching with the required focus. Self-awareness about the aspects influencing strategic thinking is crucial for effective coaching, so reflect on your beliefs, mindset, and how past experiences might affect your coaching of key strategic skills.

Communicating the goals and business drivers

Ensure that each member of your team comprehends your organization's corporate and functional strategy, high-level departmental goals, and priorities.

This foundational knowledge is crucial for them to be strategic in their roles, as it helps them stay focused on what truly matters for the organization.

To facilitate this, consider three key actions:

1. Establish a regular schedule for conveying the company's vision and strategy, with the vision representing the company's future aspirations and the strategy outlining how to achieve them. Begin with the overarching corporate strategy, encouraging discussions about its implications for your team. Check if your team members understand the cascading strategies of the departments they interact with. The frequency of these conversations depends on your industry's pace of change.

2. Communicate corporate-level priorities and clarify the connection between your department's priorities and these broader organizational goals. This alignment helps your team recognize how their daily work contributes to the organization's larger purpose.

3. Educate your team about the distinction between pursuing revenue or profit and pursuing value creation for the company. When team members grasp the value drivers of the business—such as customer, employee, and supplier value drivers—it paves the way for sustainable profit. This knowledge is rooted in a deep understanding of customer needs and consideration of all key stakeholders in the business. Encourage everyone on your team to understand and contribute to this essential aspect.

Start by identifying your meeting schedule and booking meetings throughout the year. Summarize the company and department vision and strategy for your team. Invite key stakeholders to share their goals and priorities with your team, and provide them with articles on value creation and value drivers to offer a broader perspective. These steps are excellent starting points to enhance your team's strategic understanding.

Setting an example with a self-assessment

As a manager or leader, it is crucial to lead by example and practice the skills you aim to reinforce in others. To assess your current example-setting, consider the following questions regarding your own strategic thinking and actions:

1. Understanding the Company's Vision and Strategy:

- How well do you grasp your company's vision and strategy? Can you easily summarize them on a single page?

- Have you compared your understanding with that of your peers? Address any conflicting responses to enhance clarity.

2. Knowledge of Value Drivers:

  - Are you well-versed in your company's value drivers, and do you effectively communicate them?

  - Think about how Amazon prioritizes convenience. Can you list your organization's value drivers and rate them relative to competitors?

3. Environmental Scanning:

  - Do you regularly gather information to gain an early understanding of internal and external trends and new business opportunities?

  - Demonstrating the importance of environmental scanning will encourage your team to follow suit.

4. Encouraging Differing Perspectives:

  - How well do you promote diverse viewpoints within your team? Do you encourage team members to share their perspectives and consider alternative views?

  - Are you curious and inclined to explore questions before providing answers?

5. Carving Out Time for Strategic Thinking:

  - Do you allocate time for strategic thinking, and does your calendar reflect the organization's current strategic priorities?

  - Is your communication style aligned with that of a strategic thinker, or have you received feedback about being overly detailed?

6. Comfort with Influencing and Challenging the Status Quo:

  - Are you comfortable gaining buy-in from peers, spearheading changes within the organization, and taking calculated risks?

  - Recognize your strengths and weaknesses to determine when to involve colleagues in the coaching process.

By assessing your own strategic abilities, you can better guide and support your team, ultimately benefiting both your development and theirs.

Preparing for roadblocks

Preparation before coaching your team on strategic thinking is essential, as it may pose unexpected challenges. When your team begins asking more questions and challenging your ideas, your initial reaction might be defensiveness. However, it is crucial to value developing strategic abilities in others over the comfort of having all the answers. Supporting your team's strategic development also requires embracing risk-taking. Creating a competitive advantage entail choosing innovative and different approaches, which involves some level of risk. Rather than penalizing team members who take appropriate risks, we should reward their contributions.

Becoming more strategic may introduce ambiguity initially. Considering various trends may require planning for multiple scenarios, and incorporating diverse perspectives can lead to conflicting views. Acknowledging these challenges upfront and persevering through the initial discomfort will lead to productive discussions, better decision-making, increased profitability, and long-term organizational advantage.

Curating the internal signals

To develop effective strategies and strategic leadership, it is essential to start by coaching your team to observe and analyze data, signals, and trends in their environment. While external factors like market trends and competitors are important, internal signals are often overlooked. Here are some tips to help your team understand the significance of tracking internal trends and establish practical approaches:

1. Emphasize that observing trends is an integral part of their job, not an extra task. Include it in performance reviews and remind them during one-on-one meetings. The level of effort may vary depending on the business context, but consistent effort is expected.

2. Define the types of data they should be aware of. Encourage them to identify trends in their daily work, such as changes in interactions with internal partners or technology performance. The goal is to capture data relevant to their unique vantage points on strategic issues.

3. Stress the importance of monitoring meaningful data, whether it represents opportunities or threats. Encourage the curation of carefully chosen, thoughtful data that provides valuable insights.

4. Align data gathering with each team member's personality style. Introverts may prefer data-driven research, while extroverts may opt for conversations with colleagues.

5. Establish the habit of curating signals by assigning exercises to track trends. Dedicate specific time each week or month to stay updated on these trends and use one-on-one meetings to discuss observations and their potential implications for the business.

Coaching your team on identifying meaningful data and developing the discipline to monitor the internal environment is crucial for effective strategic leadership.

Curating the external signals

Strategic thinking necessitates a strong understanding of external factors. Effective strategic thinkers regularly scan and track external forces to avoid insular thinking and wasted resources. They read competitor reports, stay updated with industry journals, and engage with external experts and partners.

Managing the overwhelming amount of external data can be achieved by coaching your team to use frameworks like PESTEL (political, economic, social, technological, environmental, legal). By assessing trends in these areas and their impact on their roles or the business, your team can identify emerging issues.

Encourage your team to look for early signals of future opportunities and threats, such as insights from research journals, articles, or blogs by experts in the field. They should curate these signals by tracking key experts and maintaining a shared document of takeaways.

Creating an external benchmark dashboard is also helpful. Ensure your team sets up a routine for keeping it up to date and holds periodic discussions on emerging issues and trends. This approach fosters strategic thinking and innovation by breaking free from echo chambers.

Building inquiry skills

Fostering inquiry skills is fundamental for strategic thinking. To develop these skills in your team, create a culture that not only welcomes but encourages asking questions. Here are some steps to nurture curiosity in your team:

1. Lead by example: Start asking strategic questions yourself, setting the expectation as a leader. This will inspire your team to do the same.

2. Promote question-driven thinking: When your team presents solutions, ask them about the questions they considered. Use team meetings to brainstorm questions that can enhance their understanding of key business problems.

3. Diversify question categories: Encourage your team to explore various types of questions, such as database questions (data consistency), temporal questions (future outlook), and options-related questions (alternative paths or value addition).

4. Balance inquiry skills: Challenge your team to ask questions that address both the factual and practical aspects of an issue, including budget implications and team sentiments.

5. Challenge assumptions: Encourage your team to question and uncover assumptions, which can expedite strategic discussions and decision-making.

Building curiosity in a team may be challenging, as individuals often seek confirmation of their existing beliefs. Strong leaders create a safe environment for asking questions and being open to being wrong, fostering a culture of curiosity that benefits both team members and the business.

Taking multiple perspectives

To enhance your team's strategic thinking, help them sharpen four perspectives:

1. Zoom In/Zoom Out Lens: Encourage your team to switch between big-picture thinking and detailed observation. Foster this dual perspective by balancing meeting agendas with discussions on both the broader context and operational details.

2. Stakeholder Lens: Ensure your team considers the views of key stakeholders from the beginning. Make stakeholder lists visible and integrate interactions into project status reports to avoid alienating stakeholders who feel left out.

3. Temporal Lens: Train your team to think about the impact of time by brainstorming questions related to different timeframes. This lens helps anticipate future needs and adapt to changes.

4. Context Lens: Urge your team to evaluate their current operating environment and how it influences their choices and decisions. Adapt strategies and actions based on the context, which may vary in crisis situations or within different organizational cultures.

Regularly focus on these four lenses to help your team become more thoughtful in their work and decision-making processes.

Moving from information to insights

To transform information into valuable insights and foster strategic thinking in your team, consider the following strategies:

1. Daily Interactions: Train your team to interpret data and focus on the key points in their presentations. Encourage them to synthesize their takeaways from meetings during daily discussions.

2. Utilize Frameworks: Introduce frameworks like PESTEL, Five Forces, SCAMPER, or others to organize and expand their thinking. Encourage them to ask, "So what?" to uncover the potential impact of findings.

3. Scenario Planning: Engage your team in scenario-planning exercises. Have them create best-case, moderate-case, and worst-case scenarios around challenges and discuss potential implications and actions for each scenario.

These skill-building exercises can help your team develop meaningful insights, facilitating their transition from information to strategic thinking. Start by incorporating these practices today to observe the difference in your team's thinking.

Build skills and behaviors

Developing strategic thinking skills requires more than just tasks like frameworks and scenario planning. It also involves essential behavioral practices:

1. Creating Mental Space: Coach your team to make time for creative thinking by disconnecting from busyness. Encourage them to find inspiration in moments of solitude, like a walk or a quiet break.

2. Collaborative Idea Exchange: Emphasize that insights are not solitary endeavors. Team members should come together in small groups to bounce ideas off each other and improve their thinking collectively.

3. Avoiding Cognitive Traps: Help your team recognize and avoid common thinking traps like confirmation bias, overestimating positives, and an impulse for immediate action. Exercises like scenario planning can aid in countering these biases.

By combining these behavioral practices with strategic thinking skills, your coaching efforts become more impactful and transformational. Encourage your team to be aware of these practices and common thinking traps to foster lasting improvements in their strategic thinking abilities. Display a list of important behaviors as a reminder in your workspace.

Using your time strategically

One common obstacle to being strategic is a lack of time. To address this, coach your team in these four key areas:

1. Mindset Shift: Help your team realize that they don't have to choose between daily tasks and strategic thinking. They can balance both to support the organization's strategic goals.

2. Time Understanding: Assess how your team currently uses their time. Identify the portion spent in meetings, operational tasks, and strategic activities. Then, have them define their ideal time allocation for better balance.

3. Creating Space: Encourage your team to eliminate non-essential meetings, scale back frequencies, and set aside dedicated time for thinking and planning. Regularly clean up their calendars and designate "meeting-free" days.

4. Time Management Practices: Coach your team in effective time management, including focusing on single tasks, minimizing multitasking, scheduling specific email-checking times, blocking out dedicated thinking time, and identifying their most productive hours.

By coaching these skills, your team can find more time and discipline to engage in meaningful strategic work.

Communicating strategically

Strategic thinking involves more than just understanding and making choices; it also requires effective communication. Help your team develop the skills needed to sound strategic by coaching them in these areas:

1. Structure and Succinctness: Encourage them to organize their ideas logically, group similar concepts, and prioritize them for clarity. Emphasize the importance of a structured approach to strategic conversations that begins with issue identification, builds understanding, and then delves into framing and designing solutions.

2. Eliminate Filler: Coach them to remove unnecessary filler words and phrases, avoid over-explaining, and practice delivering concise, bullet-pointed messages. Planning talking points in advance can prevent rambling and keep the message on track.

3. Framing: Teach the art of framing ideas by providing context or sharing stories that illuminate the idea and its implications. Encourage your team to explore different framing choices before settling on an approach to ensure better understanding and alignment.

By coaching these communication skills, your team can effectively convey their strategic thoughts, leading to better outcomes and understanding within the organization.

Coaching to challenge the status quo

Becoming more strategic often involves asking challenging questions and challenging the status quo, which can lead to defensive reactions from others. To help your team handle these situations effectively, consider the following strategies:

1. Speak to Possibilities: Encourage your team to focus on possibilities rather than taking fixed positions. By avoiding rigid stances and embracing potential outcomes, they can reduce defensiveness and resistance to new ideas. For example, instead of expressing concern about missing funding in the budget, they can frame questions around addressing upcoming challenges and exploring how additional funding could be beneficial.

2. Focus on Assumptions: Teach your team to delve into the assumptions underlying recommendations. By understanding the root causes of a person's thinking, they can engage in more substantive discussions. Encourage a "tell-me-more" approach to uncover the reasons behind current practices and their alignment with future goals.

3. Embrace Debate: Have your team reflect on their comfort with conflict and debate. Consider how their upbringing and workplace environment have influenced their ability to handle conflicting ideas. Teach them best practices for difficult conversations, such as addressing issues with facts, discussing potential impacts, seeking to understand others' perspectives, brainstorming solutions collaboratively, and reaching common agreements on the way forward.

4. Overcoming Fear of Being Wrong: Encourage your team to recognize when the fear of being wrong prevents them from engaging in debates. Encourage them to confront this fear and push through it. With practice, they can become more adept at embracing debate and contributing to a culture that objectively assesses itself and discusses strategic ideas effectively.

By implementing these strategies, your team will develop the skills necessary to challenge the status quo and engage in productive discussions, ultimately contributing to a more strategic and open-minded organizational culture.

Build a team of strategists

To take it a step further, consider the potential impact of fostering a culture of strategists within your entire department or organization. Imagine the benefits of everyone aligning on top priorities, consistently seeking relevant information, engaging in insightful conversations, and effectively sharing those insights. Creating a team and culture of strategists can truly transform your organization, leading to market excellence and differentiation – the ultimate goals of your strategic efforts.

Chapter 5 Coaching Virtually

How to build trust virtually

Coaching is like rocket fuel for careers, and its active ingredient is trust. In the virtual world, trust-building can be more challenging. To build trust remotely, consider the following do's and do not:

1. Get to know your employees: Invest in small talk, ask about their personal lives, career aspirations, and goals. Proactively support these aspirations, showing that you care about their well-being.

2. Reveal your humanity: Share your imperfections and personal experiences, as it makes you more relatable and likable to your employees, which fosters trust.

3. Be consistent: Consistently follow through on commitments, maintain emotional stability, and keep your promises, so your employees can rely on you. Inconsistency erodes trust.

Do not badmouth others: Avoid speaking negatively about people, especially your employees' peers, as it can raise doubts about your trustworthiness.

Remember these principles to effectively build trust while working remotely.

Coaching conversations you can have virtually

Effective coaching does not require you to be an all-knowing expert. To be a great coach, focus on building trust, invest time, ask probing questions, and provide your perspective when appropriate. Consider three main coaching conversation types:

1. Coaching to Solve Problems: Help employees think more proactively and suggest improvements. Frame behavior corrections as a step in their development journey.

2. Development Coaching: Assist employees in working towards their goals and aspirations. Periodic coaching sessions help track progress and assess what's effective or not in their process.

3. Career Coaching: Guide employees in planning their career progression, such as building essential skills and making strategic moves to reach their desired positions.

Remember that coaching does not have to be formal and can include shorter, informal "coaching snacks" to provide your employees with timely attention. Since remote work does not naturally facilitate coaching, be intentional about integrating coaching conversations into your schedule.

Use the GROW model to coach virtually

Managers often avoid coaching due to uncertainty and time constraints, especially in remote situations. The GROW model simplifies the process. Here is a breakdown:

- G for Goal: Ask your employee about their career or situation-related goals. Clarify the goal's specifics by asking about interim steps and criteria for achievement.

- R for Reality: Discuss the current situation and what is working well. Identify the gap between the current state and the goal.

- O for Options: Engage in an open conversation about various approaches to bridge the gap. Encourage exploring potential solutions.

- W for Way Forward: Focus on decision-making and next steps. Inquire about their action plan, when to check progress, and how you can support them.

The GROW model empowers you to facilitate goal achievement and development for your employees.

Coaching virtually for career mobility

A leading reason for employee turnover is the lack of a clear career path or growth opportunities. This issue becomes even more challenging in remote work situations. As a manager, it is crucial to incorporate career mobility coaching into your virtual coaching practices. While it may seem counterintuitive because you want to retain talent, helping employees plan their career path within the company is ultimately in your best interest. It builds your reputation as a talent developer and fosters a culture of retaining strong talent.

Here is how you can guide your employees in creating their career path:

1. Assess their current strengths and weaknesses.

2. Discuss their interests and aspirations, offering ideas and options.

3. Help them identify the required skills and experiences.

4. Encourage networking and introductions to relevant contacts.

5. Assist in creating a written plan with specific dates and commitments.

6. Ensure regular check-ins to track progress.

By demonstrating a genuine interest in your employees' careers, even if it leads them elsewhere, you enhance your reputation as an effective virtual manager.

Master listening while virtual

How you appear while listening on video is crucial in remote coaching situations. In-person interactions allow for more natural nonverbal cues, but with remote communication, your facial expressions and body language must be consciously managed to convey your attentive listening. To come across as a listener in video conversations, follow these steps:

1. Position your camera at eye level and maintain direct eye contact. Looking down or away from the camera can signal disinterest or distraction, while eye contact demonstrates active listening.

2. Adjust your facial expressions by smiling, nodding, and leaning in slightly. Since video expressions tend to be less pronounced, it's essential to accentuate these nonverbal cues to convey your engagement. It might feel unusual initially, but it is a skill worth practicing.

3. Implement paraphrasing and mirroring. Reflecting back what someone has said shows that you're actively listening, and it allows the other person to confirm or clarify their message. Paraphrasing provides a moment for the speaker to contemplate their words and ensure they accurately convey their thoughts.

Incorporate these practices not only during coaching sessions but in all interactions with your team to demonstrate your attentive listening skills effectively.

Find informal coachable moments while virtual

Generating informal coaching opportunities in a remote work environment requires creativity and intentionality. Here are some strategies you can employ:

1. Utilize chat or instant messaging (IM) for casual contact. Initiate a quick voice chat by asking if your employee has a few minutes for a conversation. Use this as an opportunity to share positive observations and build on their progress. For instance, praise their recent performance and express your interest in how others can benefit from their skills.

2. Set up virtual coffee or a "walk and talk" session. Instead of sitting in your usual environments, you and your employee can take your phones and go for a walk while having a conversation. This change of scenery can lead to deeper dialogues and added privacy.

3. Establish virtual office hours. Invite your employees to join open video sessions for informal discussions. Encourage them to initiate these interactions by sending out prompts, such as professional or personal topics to discuss during the sessions.

By incorporating these creative approaches to informal coaching moments, you and your employees can make virtual coaching just as accessible and effective as traditional in-person interactions.

Use the COIN model to give feedback virtually

Feedback is a crucial aspect of employee growth and development, especially in a remote work environment. Many managers may feel uncomfortable providing feedback remotely, but it is essential to help your employees progress in their careers. To simplify the feedback process, consider the COIN model, which stands for Context, Observable facts, Impact, and Next steps:

1. Context: Begin by setting the context, describing the situation or environment in which the feedback is relevant.

2. Observable facts: Base your feedback on specific, observable facts that you've personally witnessed. Instead of vague statements, use concrete examples to convey your point.

3. Impact: Explain the impact of the observed behavior or action on others, projects, or outcomes. Make it clear why the feedback is necessary.

4. Next steps: Encourage your employees to think about how they can address the feedback and ask for their suggestions. If needed, offer constructive suggestions for improvement.

Using the COIN model for feedback will help you provide more meaningful and effective feedback in a remote work setting, aiding your employees in their professional development.

Help your employees construct coaching action plans, virtually

Coaching action plans are not just paperwork. They are a practical tool to help employees turn their dreams into reality. You can guide your employees in creating action plans to achieve their goals. Start by defining a specific goal, such as a promotion or skill development within a given timeframe.

For instance, if an employee aims to become a manager, identify the necessary skills like project ownership and team management. They can take actions like handling projects independently and offering help to peers to practice management skills.

To measure success, consider indicators such as peers seeking their guidance or the employee asking more strategic questions. Establish clear timeframes with milestones to track progress effectively. Utilize coaching action plans to support your employees in making their dreams a reality.

Virtually coach employees who are resistant to your coaching

Dealing with employees who resist coaching can be challenging. Two common types are Francine, who avoids coaching, and Eddie, who becomes defensive. When working remotely, it is essential to adjust your approach.

Start by reflecting on your coaching style. Ask trusted peers or employees for feedback to ensure you're perceived positively. Adjust your approach if necessary.

If your employees understand your good intentions, consider a more informal method like a phone call "walk-and-talk" where you get to know them better, address their concerns, and build rapport.

Alternatively, focus on their strengths to engage resistant individuals positively. Create a team ritual of periodic strength sessions to enhance the overall atmosphere and improve your coaching effectiveness.

Keep experimenting with tactics to unlock resistant employees' potential and remember not to take their resistance personally. Adapt to their needs and find ways to connect with them.

Coaching top performers virtually

Star employees are exceptional, but they still require attention and coaching. Neglecting them, especially when working remotely, can lead to disinterest or attrition. To effectively coach high performers, follow these steps:

1. Get to know them personally: Understand their motivations and career aspirations to tailor your coaching.

2. Challenge them: Collaboratively set stretch goals to keep them engaged and growing. Goals should align with their unique desires, whether skill-building or goal achievement.

3. Encourage mentorship: Help them find mentors, individuals ahead in their careers who can provide valuable advice and guidance.

Coaching high performers is vital to maintain their enthusiasm and continued growth, so invest in their development.

Practice your skills

After covering various aspects of virtual coaching, it is time to put your learning into practice. Choose one skill such as having career coaching conversations, using the GROW model, implementing the COIN model for feedback, enhancing trust and rapport, improving active listening, adjusting your approach to resistant employees, or coaching high-performing employees. Select just one skill, schedule when you will use it, and practice it consistently for a few weeks. Over time, you will develop your virtual coaching expertise.

Chapter 6 Coaching New Managers

Think differently: Aspects of the manager's mindset

Teaching new managers to serve as multipliers means they can achieve exponential results, including significantly reducing their time spent on management tasks. Here are five different "mindset hats" to help new managers transition effectively:

1. Manager as Coach: Instead of giving direct orders, encourage them to ask open-ended questions that empower their team members to think critically.

2. Manager as Thought Partner: Urge them to challenge team members and stimulate creative thinking by questioning assumptions, fostering innovation, and making the team's collective ideas more significant than the sum of its parts.

3. Manager as Advocate: Teach them to actively support their team members within the organization, ensuring their work is recognized and helping them advance.

4. Manager as Mirror: Advise them to highlight team members' strengths, providing specific feedback to promote self-awareness, both in regular feedback and on specific projects.

5. Manager as Teacher: Emphasize that they can save time and energy by sharing their knowledge and expertise directly, especially during key teaching moments.

These five mindsets offer a foundation for new managers to become multipliers. Consider which additional "multiplier mindset hats" align with your onboarding and management process. Successful managers adopt a different approach to their work compared to non-managers. They focus on achieving outcomes and broader impact rather than individual contributions. Encourage your new manager to work on the team toward a strategic vision.

Foster early trust between your new manager and their team

A crucial aspect of helping your new manager begin successfully is assisting them in developing genuine early relationships with their direct reports. Just because someone becomes a manager does not automatically make them more knowledgeable or intelligent than their team members. Your new manager might share these sentiments during their transition.

Recommend your new manager meet one-on-one with their direct reports, ideally in an informal setting to establish connections and trust. Encourage them to set expectations early:

- Define what success means for the team.

- Identify their team's key strengths.

- Recognize their personal values and strengths as a leader.

- Communicate what's essential to convey to team members.

- Establish preferred communication and collaboration methods, like meeting schedules or communication platforms.

Incorporate a mutual feedback process. Suggest your new manager to ask their team "What do you expect from me as your new manager? What worked and did not work with your prior manager?" This promotes trust from the outset and provides valuable insights for navigating team dynamics effectively.

Debunk new manager doubts: Help build confidence

Imposter syndrome, a common experience for managers, especially those entering a new role, involves feeling like you might not belong or that your success is due to luck. It often includes a fear of being exposed as a fraud. When new managers, especially those early in their careers compared to their team members, take on additional responsibilities, self-doubt can emerge.

When onboarding new managers, addressing emotional and cultural dynamics is equally essential alongside tactical responsibilities. Other common doubts or myths new managers might experience include the need to have all the answers, being more skilled than their direct reports, age and experience-related concerns, fear of not being heard, and the fear of work not being done correctly without their direct involvement. In these situations, emphasize vulnerability and share your own transition experiences, help your new manager recognize their strengths, and instill confidence while acknowledging the emotional ups and downs.

Transparency about your own mistakes and ongoing learning, and the acknowledgment that nobody has everything figured out, creates an environment where new managers can learn through experience, even if they make mistakes along the way.

Plant: 90-day and one-year vision setting for new managers

The first stage, "plant," focuses on strengths and one-year vision. You can help new managers by asking questions like: What tasks and projects energize them the most? How can they leverage their strengths from their prior role into their new leadership position as they manage others? Encourage them to visualize their one-year vision: What does success look like in their new role as a people manager in the first three months? What new skills do they need? What impact do they hope to achieve, and what specific outcomes are expected? For example, I guided a team member transitioning to a managerial role to approach her assignments proactively and strategically, with weekly updates that included both her projects and her management responsibilities.

Scan: Adjust the three management levers

In the second stage, "scan," after guiding your new manager through uncovering strengths and setting their one-year vision, you can collaborate on identifying three key elements for their 90-day or six-month onboarding plan: people, skills, and projects.

1. People: New managers should ask themselves questions like, can they coach their team members effectively, aligning their strengths with the team's needs? Can they attract and hire top talent and manage performance, addressing issues like a toxic work environment? For example, I once had a manager who excelled at strategy with senior leaders but created a culture of burnout among her direct reports, highlighting the importance of prioritizing people and their well-being.

2. Process: While a manager may be adept at coaching, without effective norms, systems, and processes for collaboration, their team's efficiency can suffer. Creating documents like a manager manual and operating principles can make processes transparent and replicable, reducing friction and promoting consistency.

3. Purpose: Ensuring that team members understand success and work towards a common goal helps prevent conflict and confusion. Documenting operating principles can provide insight into the company's purpose and how the manager approaches problem-solving at a high level, enabling team members to adapt and solve new problems independently.

Empower your new manager to develop their leadership skills in these three areas during their onboarding journey.

Pilot: Set small experiments to help new managers acclimate

The third stage involves identifying small experiments to work on with your new manager as they establish rapport with their team and develop leadership skills. Pilots and experiments create psychological safety by allowing them to test new projects before fully committing.

For example, a common pilot for new managers, even before they have official direct reports, is leading a project where their distributed team members report to them in a dotted-line capacity. Another pilot might involve a team lead managing day-to-day operations while you and the new manager share responsibilities, such as handling performance reviews. This approach helps model complex processes and creates a safe environment for them to manage the team.

Additional pilot ideas for new managers include attending relevant courses, shadowing a respected manager during one-on-one meetings (with the direct reports' consent), reading recommended leadership books, and brainstorming experiments to try with their team, such as creative team-building exercises. The key is to encourage them to develop their own leadership style, building confidence both in themselves and their team's confidence in their ability to learn and improve.

When setting up pilots for new managers, focus on finding tasks that are challenging but not overwhelming. The goal is to build their confidence in managing others and their team's confidence in their capacity to learn and grow.

Launch: Wrap new manager coaching

The fourth stage is "Launch," and it can be seen as both a "Big Launch " and a "Little Launch".

A "Big Launch" launch refers to going all-in on a new direction after conducting a series of small experiments or pilots. Your new manager has just experienced a "Big Launch " launch by taking on their new role, transitioning from an individual contributor to a people manager. This transition is a significant paradigm shift and can be challenging. Acknowledging the learning curve and potential discomfort can help ease your new manager's journey. Encourage them to accept mistakes as part of the learning process and to seek feedback along the way.

A "Little Launch " launch occurs within a single coaching conversation and focuses on closing the meeting with specific questions:

1. What's one insight or "aha" moment from this conversation?

2. What's one small next step they can take in the next week?

3. What one next step would have the most significant impact?

4. A final accountability question, such as "What will you do, by when, and how will I know?"

Over time, your coaching conversations with your new manager will likely shift from discussing logistics and people management processes to more nuanced discussions about nurturing the unique strengths of each team member. These conversations may also involve coaching through challenging situations and difficult conversations with team members.

Celebrate your new manager's successes and provide ongoing encouragement and support during their transition. Consider setting future milestones and recognizing their achievements along the way.

Empower new managers with these three coaching strategies

Distinguishing between managing and coaching is crucial. Managing involves setting a clear vision and strategy. As a manager, your role is to set metrics, provide guidance, and ensure deliverables align with the vision.

Coaching, however, emphasizes deep listening and asking powerful questions, without a predetermined endpoint. By asking new or unconsidered questions, you help individuals think differently, fostering new neural pathways. Instead of providing direct answers, you facilitate their expertise and critical thinking.

Encourage your new manager to begin with a coaching approach, asking team members, "What do you recommend, and why?" It is more empowering and promotes learning. When a single correct answer is evident, provide it directly to save time.

To help your new manager, suggest that they pause before answering questions from their team. Team members should think of potential solutions and recommendations, promoting critical thinking.

Lastly, when conducting meetings, advise your new manager to avoid taking notes during conversations, as it can imply that they have or need all the answers, break eye contact, and make the other person self-conscious. Trust that both parties will remember key points, and summarize them after the conversation ends. Encourage your new manager to adopt this practice for more meaningful interactions.

Help new managers avoid bottlenecks

Many of us have emails languishing in our inboxes, some unanswered for weeks, causing indecision or hesitation. In the same way, new managers may inadvertently become bottlenecks for their teams. Just like your to-do list, they might accumulate tasks, leaving team members waiting for their input, reducing efficiency, and hindering strategic work. A bottleneck is a single or limited resource that constrains the performance of an entire system.

When onboarding a new manager, it is crucial for them to recognize and resolve bottlenecks. Help your new manager identify tasks only they can do and delegate the rest, empowering their team to suggest solutions. By recognizing tasks, they can delegate using the "Five T's" (tiny, tedious, time-consuming, terrible at, and teachable), they can focus on high-value tasks. Encourage them to track their daily activities and allocate time to where they are most needed, ensuring optimal results.

Stay connected beyond the transition

Regular formal and informal career check-ins are essential for new managers, especially in the early stages. These conversations provide an opportunity to discuss challenges and development areas that relate to the new manager's broader career goals.

Start these conversations by creating psychological safety and assuring that your goal is to assist, not judge. Practice active listening, allowing the new manager to share their strengths and aspirations. Provide your input and advice at the end, as you want them to model for their team that you are a guide and resource, not the sole expert.

Discuss what proved more challenging or easier than expected to align expectations and experiences. By remaining open, vulnerable, and transparent about your own experiences, you encourage your managers to do the same with their teams. Learning continues as we navigate the complexities of building strong work relationships.

Chapter 7 Coaching New Hires

Create a new hire onboarding checklist

When welcoming a new employee to your team, it is essential to cover four main areas. The first is the company level, including culture, processes, communication tools, acronyms, terminology, and necessary technology. The second is specific to your team, encompassing your team's culture, work style, and unique technologies or processes. The third is interpersonal relationships within the team and with cross-functional teams, encouraging interactions and introductions. The fourth involves the individual goals of the new employee, understanding their motivation, interests, and learning needs. To efficiently onboard, create a plan to address each category, either in one-on-one meetings or with the help of team members. A three-month onboarding period is a good starting point, but adjust it as needed based on your team's specific needs. Consider using post-onboarding surveys to collect feedback and continuously improve the process.

Integrate new hires by creating a context for coaching

Instead of merely instructing a new hire on what to do, consider a coaching approach to onboarding. This approach involves co-creating the onboarding process, with regular check-ins to gather their input. In the initial month or two, conduct frequent check-ins, at least once a week, preferably twice. These sessions help the new hire organize their questions and concerns. Start by discussing their background, both professionally and personally, and explore their strengths and interests that might be relevant to the role. Encourage them to share their passions, even if they do not seem directly related to their job. These interactions can reveal hidden strengths and connections. During check-Ins, review their progress and identify what is working well and what areas need improvement. Engage in problem-solving discussions to address any challenges they might be facing.

Quick wins: Empower your new hire to make an impact

New team members, especially those new to your company, may experience emotional ups and downs as they adjust to the challenges of learning new processes, terminology, and interpersonal dynamics. To ease their transition and reduce overwhelm, focus on achieving three to five quick wins within their first week, first month, and first three months. These small accomplishments will help build their confidence and momentum. When coaching them on these quick wins, ask about the significance of each milestone and what success should look like. You can consider involving them in tasks beyond onboarding logistics, such as creating operating principles or philosophies for your team. The coaching approach to onboarding emphasizes open dialogue, feedback, and exploration in addition to clear instructions.

Plant: 90-day and one-year vision for onboarding success

To prepare for what's next in your role, the four-stage process, can be a valuable framework for individuals or managers guiding coaching conversations. You can work through these stages – Plant, Scan, Pilot, Launch – flexibly, whether in 15 minutes or over a more extended period. Explaining these stages to new hires can help them navigate future challenges and conduct informal career check-ins. In the Plant stage, focus on identifying their strengths and creating a one-year vision. Find out what energizes them, what they excel at, and what they were known for in previous roles. Establish a vision for success, aiming for a year from now, or perhaps a 90-day or six-month vision, including desired skills, growth, and impact. Use open-ended questions like "What else?" and "What's important to you about that?" to explore and refine their strengths and vision, setting the stage for the next steps.

Scan: For people, skills, and projects in the new role

After identifying your new hires' strengths and their 90-day onboarding vision, the second stage is "scan." This stage is like planning a route on Google Maps, where you consider three key elements to help your new hire bridge the gap between their current state and their onboarding vision: people, skills, and projects. In the "people" category, consider assigning a buddy or friend tour to help your new hire acclimate to the team culture. Think about who else they should meet, both within your team and cross-functionally, to support their projects and integration. In the "skills" category, determine what skills your new hire will need to succeed in their role and during the onboarding process.

Map out short-term and longer-term skill development, aligning them with the vision for their first 90 days or six months. Leverage their existing strengths to prepare them effectively. Finally, consider the "projects" category, which involves brainstorming three types of projects: small, medium, and large. Small projects can quickly achieve wins and relate to the onboarding process itself. Medium projects offer opportunities for learning and skill development. The large projects align with their role and the reason you hired them, and coaching conversations are crucial to set them up for success on these significant tasks.

Pilot: Identify small experiments for your new hire to tackle while onboarding

The third stage is "pilot," which involves setting up small experiments related to the projects brainstormed during the "scan" stage. These pilots and stretch assignments create a sense of psychological safety, similar to a pilot episode of a TV show that tests whether the series should be picked up. Pilots allow for exploring smaller projects that can lead to more significant initiatives if successful, aligning with the new hire's interests, strengths, and team goals. A successful pilot helps identify three key aspects: enjoyment, expertise potential, and room for expansion. Examples of onboarding pilots include shadowing a team member for part of a day, inviting someone they have not spent much time with for a virtual lunch or coffee, or taking on projects outside of their main role.

Launch: Powerful questions to wrap new hire onboarding

The fourth stage is "Launch." In this context, it's not about introducing them to a new role, but preparing them for the role you hired them for. There are two types of launch moments to consider: "Big Launches" and "Little Launches".

A "Big Launch" launch involves fully transitioning your new hire into their role, signaling the end of hands-on guidance, and having confidence in their ability to manage their tasks and decisions. It could be assigning significant projects and deadlines or completing the central onboarding program.

A "Little Launch" launch applies to individual coaching conversations. It focuses on closing a discussion with four key questions:

1. What insights did you gain from this conversation?

2. What small step can you take in the next week?

3. What next step will have the most significant impact?

4. An accountability question like, "What will you do and how will I know?" For example, setting a deadline and reporting back.

Over time, coaching conversations will shift from familiarizing new hires with company elements to discussing project statuses, seeking guidance, or suggesting improvements. Celebrate their achievements and support their transition into their official role. Define the milestones for a "Big Launch" launch and find ways to celebrate these with the team.

Stay connected through formal and informal career check-ins

Have career conversations at least twice a year outside of the typical formal performance reviews. This approach ensures a more relaxed and open-minded atmosphere, free from performance or bonus-related pressures.

In these career conversations, the goal is not to solve problems or provide immediate advice, as managers often do by default. Instead, coaching conversations focus on using powerful questions to explore ideas further. It is like inflating an idea balloon. You listen 70% of the time, ask impactful questions 20% of the time, and spend the remaining 10% summarizing what you've heard and possibly suggesting different paths for the conversation.

The less you talk and dictate the outcome, the more your team member benefits. This approach underscores that they are the expert on their career, while you act as a guide and resource rather than having all the answers.

Encourage transparency and celebrate the inevitable mistakes in new hire onboarding

When coaching a new hire who may be hesitant to bring up concerns, it is crucial to encourage open discussions, especially regarding challenging topics such as failures and obstacles they encounter.

Creating psychological safety is essential. You should model vulnerability for your new team member to foster transparency. Celebrate moments of learning, both what they know and what they are discovering. For instance, a team member learned to appreciate making mistakes, which led to valuable insights. When facing inefficiencies or misunderstandings, it is an opportunity for learning and improvement.

It is not necessary to solve everything in one conversation; discussions and learning moments can be ongoing. Initially, you will identify values, operating principles, and chances for system and documentation enhancement. With time, new insights will continue to emerge, and you can revisit tricky topics in subsequent one-on-one sessions.

As a bonus, consider having your new hire improve onboarding documentation as they go through the process since they are best equipped to provide valuable insights and answers to questions you might not have considered.

Avoid three common coaching mistakes when onboarding new hires

When coaching, especially new hires, the power lies in simple, impactful follow-up questions rather than complex, innovative inquiries. Common mistakes include:

1. Providing too many answers: Instead of constantly offering solutions, prompt your new hire to propose their approach, share pros and cons, and draw from their previous experiences.

2. Missing opportunities for follow-up: Pay attention to shifts in their energy, tone, and enthusiasm. Ask them about what excites them and what's behind those changes to foster self-awareness.

3. Overthinking or dwelling on "should": When they are stuck on a problem or decision, inquire about their gut feeling. Encourage them to explore their head, heart, and gut responses, moving beyond societal expectations and entering the realm of whole-body intelligence.

As a manager, you can guide your team members out of overthinking and into holistic decision-making, drawing from their various intelligence centers. This approach can lead to more profound and meaningful career conversations.

Chapter 8 Coaching for Results

Five starting questions to avoid the pitfalls

Occasionally, your one-on-one conversations with coaches can become challenging. There might be issues like missed meetings or a lack of commitment to goals and accountability. In such situations, you may resort to telling people what to do in order to expedite progress. To help you avoid these pitfalls, here are five crucial questions:

1. Is your employee coachable? Not everyone is receptive to coaching, so spend your time wisely with those who are willing to engage in the process.

2. Is coaching relevant? Ensure that your why, as well as your coaches' why, align with their larger aspirations and remain compelling to keep them engaged.

3. Is it simple? Don't overcomplicate the coaching process; use one tool at a time and let it develop.

4. Is it challenging? Finding the right balance between support and challenge is essential for growth and results in coaching.

5. What structure is best? Tailor your coaching structure to the needs and goals of your coaches, whether it involves frequent check-ins or a fixed schedule for maintaining momentum and accountability. Adapt and switch things up as needed to optimize the process.

How to assess coachability

As a manager coach, your time is valuable. To make the most of it, it is important to focus your energy on coachable individuals. Coachable people possess these attributes:

1. Commitment to growth: They are enthusiastic learners who take responsibility for their personal and professional development.

2. Receptivity: Coachable individuals accept constructive criticism without defensiveness, demonstrating self-awareness and the ability to reflect on their actions and their impact on others.

3. Openness: They are willing to openly address their challenges and acknowledge the root of problems, even if they are at the center of the issue.

4. Perspective-taking: Coachable people can explore alternative ideas and approaches, integrating them into new possibilities and actions.

Have individuals you plan to coach complete it by a given deadline. Some may respond thoughtfully, while others might provide brief answers or skip questions. There may be individuals who decline to participate. While it is tempting to prioritize those who engage with the questionnaire thoroughly, it is advisable, as a leader coach responsible for your team's results, to make an extra effort with outliers. Schedule one-on-one meetings to gather answers and invest your time upfront to save time and avoid frustration later.

Create a coaching contract

When you establish a coaching relationship, it is essential to create a personalized contract to provide your coaching sessions with clear purpose, boundaries, and specificity. Here are the main elements:

1. Coaching Objectives: This section covers the objectives, milestones, success measurements, and consequences for unmet accountabilities. You should encourage your coaches to be specific, challenge uninspiring goals, and ensure alignment with team or organizational objectives.

2. Your Role as Coach: Define your role as a coach in the coaching relationship. Consider actions such as making introductions, creating special project opportunities, or securing resources for advanced training to support career development.

3. Logistics: Determine logistical details such as when, where, duration, frequency, and who initiates conversations.

4. Stakeholders: Identify relevant stakeholders, especially if you're coaching a low performer, as they may include other team members, customers, or HR. This fosters a holistic understanding of how goals and accountabilities relate to and affect key stakeholders.

Design the contract collaboratively with your coaches, viewing it as a flexible guide that can be adjusted as milestones are achieved. This ensures that your coaching work remains purposeful, challenging, and results-oriented.

Overview of support and challenge coaching

Coaching is known to enhance engagement and retention, but as a manager, you must strike a balance between limited resources and the need for results. To achieve this balance, combining two coaching strategies, supportive coaching and challenging coaching, is crucial. These strategies can be applied to three types of coaches: careerists, low performers, and high performers.

- Supportive coaching involves letting employees take the lead, building rapport, listening, reflecting, and asking powerful questions to generate solutions.

- Challenging coaching takes it up a notch by pushing individuals out of their comfort zones to confront issues, take risks, and achieve aspirational goals.

According to the book "Challenging Coaching," finding the right equilibrium between supportive coaching and challenging coaching is the key to driving performance. This is illustrated through the challenge-support matrix:

- Low challenge, low support results in apathy and inertia.

- Low support, high challenge leads to stress, tension, fear, and overly competitive behaviors.

- High support, low challenge creates a comfortable but unproductive environment.

- High support, high challenge represents the ideal state for high performance.

To demonstrate these coaching levels, consider a scenario where a director of operations (Cindy) is coaching a customer support representative (Sam) with low performance:

1. Low support, low challenge: A disinterested manager and employee interaction.

2. Low support, high challenge: Shaming and stress-inducing dialogue.

3. High support, low challenge: A supportive conversation with insufficient solutions.

4. High support, high challenge: A constructive exchange where the manager acknowledges the issue, challenges the employee to explore solutions, and avoids solving the problem for them.

The goal is to strike a balance between support and challenge while decreasing the coach's dependence over time, fostering mastery and trust to achieve better results.

How to give feedback in the coaching process

Managers who embrace coaching as their management style are passionate about aiding people's growth. Growth often requires pushing individuals out of their comfort zones, risking potential disappointments or failures. Yet, a significant challenge for manager coaches is delivering feedback that challenges assumptions and safe choices, which may limit growth and results. The fear of upsetting others, creating conflict, or damaging rapport often hinders the giving of challenging or critical feedback.

To help address this tension, examine conflict response styles and discover where your growth potential lies. This approach is based on the Thomas-Kilmann conflict model, which features four conflict styles: avoid, accommodate, compete, and collaborate. Consider a situation involving Sam, a customer support employee who behaves combatively with a customer.

- Avoidance: The default approach for many, where one avoids addressing the situation, fearing conflict and hard feelings.

- Competing: Reacting confrontationally, possibly threatening job security or accusing Sam.

- Accommodating: Confronting Sam with the issues but also agreeing with him, accommodating his reasoning and behavior.

- Collaborating: The most effective approach involves giving Sam feedback on his interaction and eliciting his ideas for improving his customer support skills.

Identify your position on the conflict style model, understand your default, and practice the feedback process for better results while maintaining relationships.

Here is the feedback process:

1. State the facts: Share observations, not your interpretations. For instance, you observed Sam raising his voice, interrupting, disagreeing, and hanging up on the customer.

2. Describe the impact: Explain the consequences of these observations, such as concerns about retaining the customer or the potential recurrence of Sam's behavior. Stay objective and focus on the issue rather than making character judgments.

3. Do a reality check: Ask Sam about his perspective and how it aligns with his experiences.

4. Use coaching skills: Ensure mutual understanding and acknowledgment of each other's perspectives.

5. Agree on next steps: Collaboratively identify actionable steps and a timeline to improve Sam's customer support skills.

Becoming comfortable with giving feedback takes practice, but embracing this approach will significantly expedite your journey to achieving desired results.

Raise the stakes on accountability

Accountability seems straightforward: state what you will do, set a deadline, and report results. Yet, for exceptional results, the stakes must be raised. Take the example of Diana, an engineer aiming for a promotion. She needed to redefine her goals and accountabilities within our coaching relationship and for her organization.

In coaching, focus on three levels of accountability:

1. Personal Accountability: Begin by defining personal goals. In Diana's case, it involved coaching her team, building influential relationships, and contributing to the company's strategic direction. As a coach, it's your responsibility to keep your coaches on track with their important goals and commitments.

2. Accountability Between Coach and Coached: Address the coaching relationship itself. For instance, if someone is consistently late, you can discuss the issue, and if needed, implement tailored consequences, such as suspending remote work or delaying a promotion. These consequences should align with the specific goal.

3. Accountability to the Organization: Act as an agent of your company and its stakeholders. Uphold standards, ethics, and ensure the focus benefits both your coaches and the organization. In Diana's case, her success was tied to her team's product innovation and sales performance, which required quarterly improvements. Holding your coaches accountable on all three levels may challenge them to step beyond their comfort zones.

Whether you are conducting spot coaching or following a more formal schedule, cultivate compassionate fierceness to nurture the kind of accountability that leads to both leadership and results.

How to listen for personal and organizational growth

You are in a coaching session with your coaches, you've created a conducive environment, initiated the conversation with "What's on your mind?" and now it's time to listen. The key to achieving results more effectively and efficiently lies in your listening skills. The authors of "Co-Active Coaching" introduce the concept of level three listening, often referred to as global listening.

- Level One Listening: This is self-oriented, where you're preoccupied with personal thoughts, distractions, or how to insert your opinions.

- Level Two Listening: In this level, you focus on your coaches, paying attention to what's said, their body language, and are fully engaged in the conversation to assist them.

- Level Three Listening (Global Listening): At this level, you transcend engagement and attunement with your coaches. You tap into your intuition to discern not only what's being expressed but also what's unspoken. You extend beyond the coaches' personal goals and agenda to consider how it all relates to your organization, incorporating cues from various stakeholders and the larger system.

For instance, look at an interaction between Sam, a customer support representative, and Cindy, his boss, using level two listening:

Cindy: "Sam, you've been here six months and you should have a better handle on things. Your numbers are dismal. What can we do to turn things around?"

Sam: "I don't know. There's such a disconnect between what the customers are asking and what the documentation prescribes."

Cindy: "I get that. But given the tools you have; how do you get past your irritation and serve the client?"

While Cindy is engaging with Sam, the solution-seeking focus may miss the level three opportunity. A more level three approach may sound like:

Cindy: "Sam, you've been here six months and I'm not sure that you have the best handle on things. Your numbers are dismal. How can we turn things around?"

Sam: "I don't know. There's such a disconnect between what the customers are asking and what the documentation prescribes."

Cindy: "I'm not sure if this is heading in the right direction, but it sounds like you might have untapped skills we could leverage to improve."

Level three listening encourages you to express your intuition or "blurt" out your insights, which can accelerate problem-solving. Moreover, it allows you to be more authentic and build trust, fostering a more open and collaborative coaching relationship. Enjoy the process of listening and sharing your intuitive insights.

Guidelines for navigating performance issues

To start, there are two important realities to acknowledge. First, performance challenges are something that everyone, including yourself, may face at some point in their careers. Second, addressing poor performance is your responsibility as a manager. It is vital to determine whether the issue lies with you, your team, or both, but it often starts with your leadership. Identify common performance problems, such as subpar work quality, time management issues, absenteeism, communication problems, harassment or bullying, and customer or stakeholder complaints.

As a manager, you can proactively prevent significant performance problems by setting clear goals and expectations, providing regular feedback, acknowledging good performance publicly, and offering constructive criticism privately. When you become aware of performance issues, address them promptly. Assess your own leadership and communication skills for potential improvement. Take responsibility and reflect on your role in the situation.

Write prompts that will help you prepare for the initial performance conversation:

1. What are the objective facts regarding the issue?

2. How does your employee's performance impact the team or organization as objectively as possible?

3. What changes are necessary to resolve the problem?

Utilize these prompts to guide your thinking and construct a factual opening statement that is free of blame. Explore ten guidelines for managing both the first conversation and ongoing performance coaching:

1. Schedule a meeting, explain its purpose, and set a supportive tone.

2. Share your specific observations objectively.

3. Request input and feedback from your employee regarding your observations.

4. Encourage them to reflect on how their behavior affects the team and organization.

5. Clearly communicate the expected behavior and results.

6. Use open-ended questions to collaborate on solutions.

7. Establish a concrete action plan and document it.

8. Identify the stakeholders who need to be informed.

9. Define consequences if expectations are not met, which may be tied to bonuses, promotions, reassignments, or layoffs.

10. Establish a follow-up structure for progress check-ins to ensure continuous improvement.

To be successful in performance coaching conversations, maintain an open and positive perspective, believing that people can make changes and correct progression when needed. This perspective will help you create a supportive atmosphere focused on achieving beneficial results for yourself, your employee, and your organization.

How to coach a low performer

Addressing a low performer's performance issues can be one of the most challenging conversations for a manager. To guide you through such a conversation, Cindy, a Director of Operations at a tech firm, and her employee, Sam, a customer support representative, as they work through these difficulties. Cindy has thoughtfully prepared her opening statement, focusing on clarity, directness, and a supportive tone. This conversation showcases the use of both supportive and challenging coaching strategies to provide Sam with multiple opportunities to find solutions and enhance accountability.

Cindy emphasizes the importance of discussing performance and finding a solution, dispelling Sam's fear of termination. She appreciates Sam's technical knowledge and diplomatic customer interactions but also acknowledges instances of rudeness and increasing customer complaints. Cindy encourages open communication and a solution-oriented approach. This conversation underlines the significance of a strong team and organization.

Sam expresses frustration about the documentation's poor quality and mentions that other representatives' work bothers him. Cindy discusses the impact of this frustration on Sam's work and helps him explore strategies for overcoming it. She commits to investigating his suggestions. In the end, Sam shows interest in mentoring and wants to improve customer service.

Cindy's conversation incorporates various skills and strategies: praise, directness, objectivity, support, challenge, brainstorming, addressing assumptions, and enhancing accountability. The key takeaway is that addressing performance issues can lead to positive change and unexpected improvements, benefiting both employees and the organization.

Challenges to coaching high performers

High performers are typically self-confident, autonomous individuals who have little tolerance for mediocrity and failure. They continuously seek self-improvement and consistently strive to surpass their own goals. However, they can sometimes come across as aggressive, arrogant, or self-centered, and may overestimate their own abilities. As a coach, it is crucial to be attentive and fully engaged when working with high performers.

To coach a high performer effectively, adopt a peer-to-peer approach, regardless of your position in the organization's hierarchy. High performers expect their coach to have similar experiences, capabilities, and goals. If you are not a good match for them, it is essential to help them establish a coaching relationship with a peer or leader in the organization to ensure they receive the necessary support for their career growth.

Here are a few guidelines for both supporting and challenging high performers:

1. Set specific, challenging goals and metrics to push their limits.

2. Regularly assess the impact of your coaching relationship and adjust strategies for continuous improvement.

3. Emphasize the importance of relationships alongside their goals, as high performers can sometimes neglect nurturing key connections.

4. Encourage them to coach others, which enhances their leadership skills and strengthens the organization's coaching culture.

5. Maintain a balance between providing challenges and delivering motivating feedback to help them overcome limiting beliefs, overused strengths, and blind spots.

6. Do not forget to acknowledge and praise them, as high performers, like everyone else, appreciate being seen and recognized.

7. Respect their need for autonomy and avoid micromanaging. Know when to step in and when to step aside.

Working with high performers will improve your coaching skills, especially in handling difficult conversations. Pay attention to the challenges they take on, as they might reveal opportunities for growth in your own role.

How to coach a high performer

Effective coaching skills involve letting the coaches take the lead, asking open-ended questions, and providing support. However, relying too heavily on supportive coaching can be time-consuming, especially in a work setting, and may not align with the preferences of high-performing individuals. High-performers typically seek challenges more than support.

In the following scenario, Cindy, the Director of Operations, is coaching Martha, a senior sales manager. Martha's goal is to improve her ability to handle difficult conversations. Cindy engages in the coaching relationship by challenging Martha, using level three listening and intuition blurts, and occasionally posing leading questions.

During their conversation, Cindy encourages Martha to confront challenges within her team, particularly with Frank. The dialogue emphasizes Martha's reluctance to speak up, the erosion of trust between her and Frank, and the impact on clients and the sales team.

Cindy consistently challenges Martha, urging her to be more courageous in addressing her speaking-up goal and the issue of trust. Cindy's persistent approach encourages Martha to confront her fears and commit to a resolution, focusing on the bigger picture of building a cohesive and successful team.

In the coaching session, Cindy avoids taking sides or vilifying Frank, ensuring that the coaching remains centered on Martha and her personal growth.

The session showcases Cindy's persistence and her ability to keep Martha focused on addressing her own challenges rather than pointing fingers at others. This is a valuable approach, especially when dealing with coaches struggling with difficult interpersonal relationships.

Next steps

As a manager and coach, you hold a unique and privileged role. While your team members are ultimately responsible for their careers, they may look to you for guidance. You are not just the boss; you are a collaborator working together toward a common purpose.

Practice your coaching skills in everyday conversations, not just during one-on-one sessions. When you use coaching techniques consistently, you demonstrate how to empower, challenge, and support others. This can have a significant impact on your organization's culture.